Artistic Singing:
Its Tone Production and
Basic Understandings

by

Lloyd F. Sunderman

The Scarecrow Press, Inc.
Metuchen, N.J.   1970

For

Choral Directors and Solo Singers

and

For All Those Who Desire to Sing Better

Table of Contents

Introduction

A strong impulse for self-expression characterizes the
singer. This instinct for song expression is the impulse which
identifies the "natural singer." The great singer has the ability to
express human emotion through the propelling momentum of the
voice, an instrument which reflects the nature and condition of the
mind. It would be impossible to have an articulate singing mechanism without its being a reflection of a sensitive and imaginative
intelligence. The interpretative singer, therefore, must be
intelligent.

When an individual opens his mouth, whether in speech or
in song, he immediately reveals through the production of tone the
emotional sensitivity of his individuality. The spoken or sung word
reveals the intensity of a singer's emotional life. A study of
singers will emphasize the accuracy of this statement.

Every individual is capable of expressing some degree of
emotional intensity. Also, everyone is able to express in speech
and song that emotion which is characteristic of his personality.
It is plain that this emotional intensity is fused into the tone through
functional mind and body activity. It must be recognized that the
quality of the tone the singer produces is the medium used for
measuring emotional intensity. Both the teacher and the singer
must start with the proper tone conceptions if effective singing is
to be achieved. The resultant tone that is produced can never be
different from the emotional and physical conceptions which are
initiated by the mind and body.

By this time it is obvious that the vocal mechanism
operates as a coordinated unit. From the incidence--thinking to
sing--to the result, a beautiful singing tone, the miracle of song
is the result of a remarkable automatic tone. By automatic tonal
action we mean that action which issues forth from the mind and

vii

throat upon the incidence of the will to sing. This automatic action may not always be pleasing to the student if incorrect conceptions have been conceived in the mind.

Every tone is dependent upon the right conception. There must be a thoughtful mind-to-body movement before the tone is initiated if breathing is to be correct; pitch will be determined by the proper concentration upon the incidence of the tonal attack. Conditions conducive to bodily or muscular relaxation and resultant action must come prior to the incidence of tone; proper tonal resonation and vocal register (vocal scale) use will also be dependent upon the establishment of the correct conditions prior to the emission of sound. The verbalism of tone is the word, and it must also be a product of correct conceptions. These vehicles so necessary to the art of good singing are first a product of the mind.

The student of voice must know that it is impossible to think of all the aforementioned acts in detail prior to the singing of a tone. The consummation of all training results from a disciplined body properly responsive to the dictates of the mind. No singer just happens to sing beautifully; every facet of intelligent vocalism is actually a manifestation of intelligent study and requires disciplines.

Thus far it has been said that music is a way for the singer to express emotion. It is the barometer of thoughts and actions. If one hundred units of conception, will and emotional expression are the optimum of an individual's expressional output, then they become the effective talent units which must be trained. When he sings, his emotional release becomes the medium of expression for which those emotions may not be revealed in any other manner. The greater the artistic revelation of the singer's talent, the more effective will be his singing. Singing must become an artistic distillation of all that the singer conceives. But a singer must possess a strong urge to sing. Desire is the dynamism of artistic singing. The will to sing can be woefully misdirected if the singer fails that will by unintelligent employment of his intelligence and talent. Finally, every singer must ask himself this question, "Do I have this important quality which is absolutely essential to singing?"

Chapter I

Tone Production

Probably it is an oversimplification to state that the purpose of deliberate singing is to produce good tone. Certainly if the singer is to be effective, he must emit tone of commendable quality. In order to attain such a result, there must be superior intelligence and musicianship. These two factors, however, need to be disciplined through training if a desirable tone quality is to be realized. It is the purpose of this book to discuss the numerous aspects of this problem so that effective tone production may become a reality for the singer.

Singing is fundamentally a process of having or establishing proper vocal (tonal) conceptions. If the singer is to have a good tone he must have a proper conception of what is to be achieved and how it is to be achieved. If the approach is through physical to mental, rather than mental to physical action, the teacher and the singer must attempt to establish or induce mental controls or disciplines--those desirable conditions which will call forth a physical action which will have a salutary effect upon the singer's mechanism.

Good vocal practice must issue from the mind as well as from the body. The mechanical vocalization without proper mind direction will be for naught. The superior teacher and singer will through discriminative understandings be able to induce through mental suggestion those conditions which will create for each singer effective learning experiences. Thus the great challenge to the vocal teacher and choral director is that he will be able to discern those vocal techniques which are appropriate to good singing. This ability distinguishes the great teacher from the mediocre one.

Mental Concepts In Tone Production

No singing teacher, nor any student of singing can ever hope
to sing beautifully unless he is able to understand how the mind operates in controlling the singing mechanism. In dealing with many
voices, it is quite often perplexing to discern just what is a mental
and what is a physical cause or effect. It would appear from just
cursory observation that many individuals are confused as to just
what the conditions are which induce a given mental or physical result. In singing it would appear that it is almost impossible to conceive a physical singing result (action) without some vestige of
prior mental stimuli or origination of thought impulses. There can
be no vocal action without a prior mental concept. Thus, there
must be a concern with the nature of tonal concepts.

Singing is a science needing much intelligent study. But the
complexity of the mind humiliates our understanding of it. We are
forced to become students of cause and effect, and must be sufficiently research minded to evaluate any overt evidence which points
up any one-to-one relationship resulting in beautiful tone production.
There is no individual who is capable of stating that muscle 27 plus
muscle 62a will always result in tone concept 4,672d. We have not
fathomed the external impact of "notions about singing" upon the
singer's mind. Today great vocal teaching is often not too far re-
moved from the skillful results of the eighteenth and nineteenth-
century masters of vocal art. The great teacher thus becomes in
all his humility, due to the complexity of the problem, a student of
mental and bodily actions--through experience and patient discerning
observation, he attempts to deal with each vocal problem as he
finds it constantly in new settings. As yet, no one has the combination to know just what mental stimuli (instructional techniques) will
elicit certain precise and minutized physical singing actions. The
mind controls all physical responses of consequence involved in artistic singing. In the final analysis the voice is subservient to the
action of the mind.

Evidences of Incorrect Physical Conditions Affecting Tone Production

In order to produce a beautiful alignment and flow of tone, the singer must first establish for himself criteria for evaluating and determining just what is inimical to the production of good tone for singing. He must understand just what is wrong or impeding the realization of a bel canto tone. Too many students do not understand what they are doing.

There are many incorrect physical conditions affecting tone production. Among the more serious are: lack of tonal concentration, lack of uniformity of tonal bore, jaw rigidity, stiffness of the tongue, mouthiness of tone quality, unusual mouth conformation or formations, receding and protruding jaw, distended neck muscles, strident tone quality, lack of breath support, and poor diction.

It is impossible to conceive of the student singing a beautiful tone if he consciously or unconsciously employs any action resulting in these conditions. Naturally, if the teacher and the student can bring about the opposite actions, the singer is certain to profit vocally. Correctness is characterized by: a relaxed expression while singing, a limpid or liquid tonal flow, a steady uninterrupted flow of tone, a seeming endless flow of breath, good fundamental vowel conformations, a proper recognition of voiced consonants, a flexible body action--especially from the waistline up, and the ability to use the voice with great agility--especially noticeable in fast moving songs.

1. Lack of Tonal Concentration. A most common observation is that when students and even professional singers are vocalizing a critical listener will be able to detect considerable variation in the quality of their tone production. Usually this is due to the fact that the singer is "dreaming" and lacks the power of aural acuity in making critical evaluation of vowel forms. Being able to detect variations in vowel forms usually requires considerable study before the singer becomes expert in discriminative vowel quality detection.

The following factors are basic to good tonal concentration and uniformity of bore of tone:

1. There must be the ear of the experienced choral teacher whose
    tonal idealisms have been thoroughly established;

2. The student must have a high innate degree of aural acuity per-
    mitting him eventual development of tonal discrimination;

3. His teacher must create for the student a learning environment
    in which the student will have an opportunity of experiencing
    how to evaluate the tones he produces--he must become a
    discriminative listener;

4. Through pupil evaluation, the teacher must establish intelligent
    learning techniques which the student will understand, and
    which will effectively induce correct mental concepts which
    will be effective for each student.

2. <u>Lack of Uniformity of Tonal Bore</u>. The improper and
proper concept of tonal bore is a major criterion for determining the
eventual quality of the singing tone. Tonal uniformity is largely
achieved by the singer's conception of a tone which eventually is
sung and becomes an aural experience. Tonal bore typifies the singer's voice. When listening to a voice we must be certain that
throughout its entire singing range, it will be uniform and of good
quality. It might be said that the most common characteristic of
singing tone is that as the voice ascends the scale the singer unconsciously spreads its bore--thus affecting its quality or timbre. A
spread tone usually becomes white, harsh, breathy, or strident
(white tone is usually conceived of as being devoid of overtones,
good resonance, and is unmusical). We are familiar with the principle of instrument construction, that the size, shape, and proportion of any resonating cavity determines pitch and to a great extent
the character of the tone quality. Can the singer visualize the clarinet being effective, if every time that the instrument produces a
tone, the shape, size, and thinness of its structure would vary?
That would be tonal chaos. That is just what is being invited when
the singer constantly changes the resonating area every time he
sings a vowel, word, or phrase. The individual must remember
that he sings through his throat and not with it. Therefore, if the
proportions of the areas affected by the singing process (bore of

the singing voice) are altered while the individual is singing, tone
quality will be greatly affected.   These alterations which the singer
incorporates into his singing mechanism affect his tone production.
A study of the following diagrams should prove helpful in understanding bore alterations during the singing process.

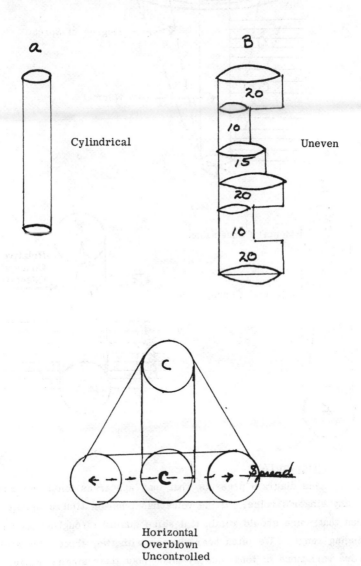

a

B

Cylindrical

Uneven

20

10

15

20

10

20

C

C

← - - → C - - - → Spread

Horizontal
Overblown
Uncontrolled

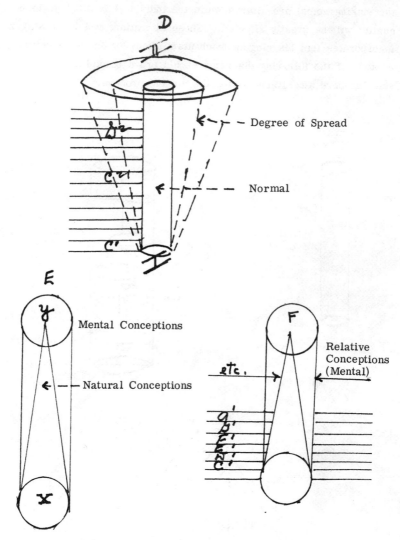

Diagram (A)

This diagram presents what may appear as tonal uniformity in any singer's voice. If the voice has inherent timbre (quality), then that voice should retain that same quality throughout its entire singing range. We often hear singers with two, three, and even more variations of tonal quality throughout their singing range. If

the inherent timbre (bore) of a voice is ten units of size, then it
becomes obvious that it cannot be fifteen in one area, twenty in another, and five in still another section of its entire singing range
and retain uniformity of quality. It can easily be appreciated that
irregularity of tonal timbre like that found in Diagram (B) would be
ruinous to the quality of any instrument whether it is instrumental
or vocal.

Diagram (B)

Whenever this occurs the tone becomes breathy, overblown,
of poor intonation, dictionally insufficient, and lacking in overtones
due to the need for better tonal focus and tonal energization. It is
certain to curtail a singer's effective tonal quality and singing
range.

Diagram (C)

This is an illustration of what happens if the tonal bore is
out of all proportion to the singer's concept as to how his voice
should sound throughout its entire range. Here we have an extreme
mouthy (tonal resonance in the mouth) situation which is devoid of
resonant reinforcement. Just because individuals produce tones with
mouth resonance does not justify the seeming naturalness of the
method or result. Much talking and breathing does not require
much more than "breath for existence" and the resultant speech or
vocalization for communication is often devoid of much mouth, jaw,
lip, and tongue action, and appropriate vowel and consonant articulation and variation. Good tone quality is dependent upon the resonance which all areas (cavities of chest and head) can contribute to
it.

Diagram (D)

Diagrammatically we illustrate the male singer, singing up the
scale one octave and a fifth. Instead of retaining the natural bore
of his tone which is designated as Concept I, he eventually spreads
his tone progressively until he has reproduced Concept II, which is
out of all proportion to his original concept. The discerning choral

teacher must train the student to become aware of what has happened to his tone when a result is created like the one in Diagram (D). It is certain that the tone will usually be flat, white, devoid of good pitch, strained, and because of its unmusical nature is certain to become unpleasant to the listener's hearing.

Diagram (E)

If the student will carefully check his tonal conceptions as he sings naturally in various sections of his vocal range, he will find that his wider conceptions are in his lower singing range and those in the upper reaches of his range are actually small and narrowed like that of a carrot tip. Therefore, if he goes from (x) to (y), he will note that this approach is more consistent with reality and actual ease of producing a tone. A properly energized vowel cannot become spread in its concept as illustrated by Diagram (D) and still retain its resonance in keeping with its inherent (natural) brilliance and beauty. A spread vowel form such as (O) in Diagram (D) is certain to become vapid and devoid of brilliance and carrying power. It has lost its inherent resonance sensation, thus the overtones may become dissipated or diffused.

Diagram (F)

This diagram indicates that the lower (chest resonance) part of the voice has the broadened concept, thus, the sonority of chest resonance is correctly found in Diagram (F). Now if the mental concept of pitch ascension is as portrayed, then we must go one step further and point out that the individual must make these mental concepts in keeping with the narrowing of the limiting nature of the eventual concepts as diagramed rather than as found in the spread concept of Diagram (D). All tone that is sung must become a correct mental concept before a proper physical result (good singing tone) can ensue.

Try this experiment. First play the topmost easily sung pitch in the singer's range. Ask him to pretend that he is going to sing the pitch, but as he is about to sing the pitch, yet retaining all accompanying sensations, he is immediately required to change

his sensations and conceive the lowest pitch in his singing range.
He must be sure to retain the high sensation while attempting to
conceive (sing) the lower. He will note that a mental conflict exists
and he will be unable to negotiate the act. Thus, if that is true for
the uppermost and lowest notes, then there must be a definite relationship existing between all the intermediary pitches between the
two points--high and low. Success depends on the absence of mental conflicts in establishing pitch sensations.

In the practice of vocalizes or in the singing of songs, all
young singers commit errors in the conception of pitch sensation
and elevation. In singing an ascending scale the student will invariably spread the bore of his tones. The voice becomes more breathy;
pitches are adversely affected; there is emphasis upon a mouthy tone
production; tone quality becomes white; some or much of the musculature of the throat and mouth becomes tightened; "neck" singing
characterizes the tonal timbre; vowel production as such is vitiated--
their tonal purity is lost because the overtones have been vitiated
and even lost.

No tone can retain its inherent lustre if the bore and resonance of the resonating chambers are being constantly changed due to
changing mouth (bore) positions. A uniformity of resonance in a
given singer's voice is dependent upon the constancy of his technical
efforts; otherwise, all of his efforts to sing tones of firmness, good
pitch, opulence and flexibility are greatly mitigated.

3. Evidences of Jaw-Rigidity. The vocalist appears to protrude the jaw in the act of singing. He is inclined to hold his jaw
rigid with little movement while singing. The mouth is usually
more closed than comfortably opened and the jaw is not relaxed.
There may appear muscular tension along the lower cheek areas as
well as evidences of tension at the outer corners of the lips. Tension in the jaw is not an isolated, but an associative action involv-
ing muscles. Usually when the lower jaw and the associated musculature with its action is rigid, the ensuing tone quality is hard
and often strident.

Suggestions for Lessening Jaw Rigidity

(a) Raise the head as in the act of drinking. In swallowing
any liquid the individual automatically relaxes the rear of the throat
in order to permit its free passage. The singer should sing with
the same throat comfort as experienced in the act of drinking the
liquid.

(b) The singer should place or lay the tongue forward in the
mouth. Its edges should touch all areas of the lower teeth. The
relaxed feeling induced by this approach to tongue action should give
the individual the feeling that the mouth feels as though it had mush
in it.

It is absolutely essential that the choral director insist that
his singers open their mouths, not with just a slit opening, but with
an aperture which is comfortably wide. The opening, of course,
must be commensurate with the structural conformation of the individual's mouth. No hard and fast rule can be established for opening of the mouth. Individuals vary and what would be a very wide
opening for one mouth might be but an average aperture to another
person. Whenever it is too open, it may induce muscular tension
and tonal stridency and hardness. If the mouth is not sufficiently
open, the tone cannot be effectively heard. Whenever the singer
produces tone through a slit mouth opening, it is likely that it will
have the affect of being blown through the nose. It may be nasal in
sound and even dull or overly covered. Such tone production is certain to result in a sound that is lifeless and emotionally expression-
less.

(c) Practice the following exercises:

Ex. 1

Nah a   Noh oh   Nah   a   Noh   oh   Nah   a   Noh
Then reverse:
Noh oh   Nah   a   Noh   o   Nah   ah   Noh   o   Näh

Be sure that the mouth is comfortably open. In singing "Nah ah," be sure that the mouth is as open on the "ah," as it is on the "Nah."

This next exercise has often proved to be helpful for loosening the jaw.

Lah, Lah, Lah, Lah, Lah, Lah, Lah, Lah, Lah, etc.
Näh, Nōh, Näh, Nōh etc.　　　up and down the scale.

When saying the "Lah," be sure that the tongue is free. Allow the jaw to sag comfortably open.

Exercise 3 employs "E-Jah" produced on two sequential pitches, as:

E jah E jah E jah E jah E jah E jah

E jah E jah E jah

Be sure that from the relatively closed mouth position in the production of "E," to the open form induced by the singing of "jah," the movement from one position is flexible and decidedly contrasted. Flexibility and looseness of jaw action are the key words in the use of these exercises.

Although we have not spoken about the sitting or standing position, breath support, tonal attack, and other physical aspects of good tone production, it is assumed that every desirable contributive singing function of which the singer is capable of producing should be employed while vocalizing these exercises.

        4. Stiffness of Tongue. The existance of this physical condition of the tongue is too frequently found among singers at nearly all stages of vocal training. It is amazing to find the many peculiar positions that a singer's tongue assumes in singing. Among the more frequently observed are the following:

        (a) The tongue is drawn posteriorly in the mouth. This affects the tone quality by muffling it, and any extreme posterior position of this organ produces what is commonly referred to as "a potato quality." Usually the singer feels a "spread sensation" at the rear of the throat with accompanying pressure on the upper area of the larynx box. Such pressure causes a rigidity of the voice box and induces an inflexibility of the singing mechanism.

        (b) The tongue is almost lengthened in its entirety, but extremely pursed in its anterior extremity. Where such a condition exists the tongue is usually rigid and tension is very pronounced in the posterior (rear) area of the organ and the condition induces varying degrees of tension in the throat. The tongue and the entire

throat area must be relaxed and flexible for free vibratory singing
action which takes place in the voice box.

(c) Tongues frequently appear seemingly curled under and
positioned high in the mid-posterior area of the mouth. The tongue
should always lie in the flat of the mouth, with the edge of the
tongue placed gently against the entire lower teeth area. Even
though the tongue position varies with the various vowel forms, it
must always remain flexible. It is a good habit to have the singer
always place the tongue gently down in the act of singing (attacking)
words. The singer should always say to himself, "Is my tongue
relaxed?" In the early stages of vocal training it would be profit-
able for the singer to have a good sized hand mirror placed in front
of him in order that he will be able to observe the position and action of the organ. Studied attention to this phase of physical organ
action while singing will prove helpful to the singer.

5. Mouthiness of Tone Quality. This is another physical
movement that is disturbing to a continuous flow of tone. Mouthiness or "munching" the tone, as it is sometimes called, refers to
an undue amount of jaw movement (closing and opening of the mouth)
while the tone is being sung.

Let us suppose that the word Dome is being held for four
(4) beats, then it is imperative that when the vowel Ō is sung, it
should be sustained without interrupting movements caused by varying movements of the jaw. Pictorially the approximate time value
given to the consonants and the vowel of the word Dome would be:

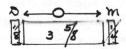

The D, a voiced-consonant, must be articulated with the resonation of which it is inherently possessed; the M, another voiced-
consonant, should be strongly resonated because it provides strong
vocal resonation for the conclusion of the word. Jaw movements
will occur whenever the resonated consonants D and M are applied
to articulation; it is the vowel that becomes the purveyor of the tone.

If the jaw moves while the vowel is being sung, the resultant tone
will be altered.

6. Unusual Mouth Conformation or Formation

(a) <u>Hair Lip</u>. This physical deformity occasionally occurs
and in severe cases does interfere with pronunciation and diction;
it may even affect tonal resonation. If the hair lip is slight in nature, however, the individual may compensate for the affected lip
conformation by making compensatory lip formation adjustments.
This will require study as to how an individual's peculiar lip affects
tone production.

(b) <u>Buckteeth and Anterior Jaw Deformities</u>. Whenever ma-
ture individuals have teeth and jaw alignments which do not permit
a good "jaw or tooth bite," the individuals need the assistance of a
good teacher and probably the professional help of an orthodontist
in attaining vocal (tonal) effectiveness. Usually specialized dental
care (and perhaps even surgery) may be needed.

(c) <u>Lip Rigidity</u>. The so called pursing of the lips very
often causes undue muscular tension and thereby adversely affects
the free emission of singing tone. It is very easy to observe the
tension either in the upper or lower lip, or both, because there are
skin creases about the lips. It should be remembered that when
the singer purses his lips, he has tension extending all the way back
to posterior facial and throat areas. Why? Because the pursed
lips always induce an attitude of straining. Any tension in the lips
would imply tension in the cheek. The singer should strive for as
much facial (cheek and lip) suppleness (relaxation) as possible. The
singer should study his mouth for its natural conformation and
strive to have it assume such a position. The teacher in striving
to solve such muscular tensions as we have described must study
the singer in order to discern why there is tense mouth and lip conformation. Frequently, nervousness will be reflected in the mouth
and lip tensions; lip quivering is frequently observable. Then, too,
tensions that are reflected in the musculature of the neck and face
are usually associated with neck singing; that is, tone which is not
adequately supported by the body. Inadequate support for any aspect

of the singing mechanism will always result in tensions. Many individuals have a tendency to contract the lips sideways. This is
just another reflection of anterior facial tensions which in these in-
stances are induced by contractions of the soft palate. Finally,
whenever the mouth looks the best and appears most natural, the
singing tone will undoubtedly be the best.

The singer should always evaluate his method of tone production on the basis of the greatest comfort that he is deriving from
his singing. If the mouth feels taut or the throat aches during singing, it is certain that the method of tone production is incorrect.
Fatigue usually accompanies tense throat singing conditions.

7. The Receding and Protruding Jaw. Individuals vary
greatly as to structural features and among them are the variations
that exist in jaw conformations. Some lower jaws recede considerably, whereas, others are more jutting, protruding, or appear to
be so structured in some people. Upon occasion it will be found
that a jaw recedes to the extent that an individual may, while singing, unduly press it upon the larynx box and neck. Each individual's
jaw needs scrutiny and recommendations for effecting good tone production must be made in keeping with the manner in which he employs his jaw while singing. If the jaw appears to protrude or jut
forward and is accompanied by a raised head position, the whole
head must be brought into alignment with a position which is helpful
to the individual while singing.

Always work for naturalness of mouth position. Get the jaw,
lips, and the entire mouth action in true alignment with the face
and head. Having the singer place the index and second finger in
the mouth will give him an idea of approximately how wide the mouth
should be opened. Overall head and specifically jaw and mouth
shape and size will indicate the amount of jaw separation or opening. Each face and head must be studied for their adaptability for
singing; individuals vary in this respect. The choral director studies the singer and the singer should be taught to observe himself
objectively in a mirror while practicing. It must be remembered
that most people speak with a jaw action which uses only a slit

mouth separation between the teeth. Try putting an object between
the teeth of the approximate width of two fingers. Very often this
will help the student get adjusted to the idea of the amount of mouth
separation. Take the object away just as soon as a good mouth
separation has been indicated to the individual. Usually tone quality
will show immediate improvement when the mouth has been adequately opened.

8. <u>Distended Neck Muscles</u>. Distended neck muscles (neck
musculature) although not frequently apparent in singers, are, when
found in a singer, evidence of extreme tension during the act of
singing. So many singers conceive the business of singing as solely a function of the throat. Even though the vocal chords are lo-
cated in the larynx of the throat, the action and support of the
whole body is necessary. If the singing mechanism above the neck-
line is supported by the body, it will be found that muscular tension
in the neck will lessen and tone quality will improve. Usually, neck
muscle distension results from lack of adequate breath support,
rigid larynx box, rigid tongue, and an assumed or rigid head position.

9. <u>Strident Tone Quality</u>. Good tone production presupposes
freedom of those muscles that are related to the process producing
a good singing tone. Freedom of muscles does not imply collapse
of musculature. If a singer is conscious of strain or tension, then
he must analyze himself in order to find out what is its cause.
The whole discussion of this section is intended toward the improvement of tone production. We believe that if the singer will correct
those physical conditions which have been listed as adversely affecting tone production he will be able to eliminate strident tone quality.
Any strain on the musculature of the throat and mouth will automatically induce "forcible pulls" which will guarantee strident tone of
poor quality. The vocal exercises which have been suggested are
designed to induce freedom of those muscles involved in the act of
singing.

Chapter II
Tone Production and Register Development

Beautiful singing tone is the objective of all singers. No one can attain the technique for producing correct singing tone unless there are clear understandings about how to achieve those mental and physical conditions which will induce correct tonal conceptions and effective singing tone.

The vibrations which eventually resonate in all the cavities of the cheek, neck, and head act as baffles and aid in resonance. They must be considered as an integral part of the consummated function--tone production. Thus, vibrations and what happens to them are of great concern to the singer.

A vibration is a product of a vibrating medium (vocal chords). Vibrations resonate and this resonation results in vocal sounds. It is the nature or quality of these sounds with which the choral singer is so vitally concerned. It must be emphasized that resonance becomes tone; consequently, all aspects of its impact upon the effectiveness of the singing voice must be studied. Finally, the intelligent use of resonance in the development of good singing tone is certain to play an important part in assisting the singer in conveying ideas and emotions.

Organic Considerations

It is the cavities in the upper torso, neck, and head that aid in the production of resonance. These cavities are: chest, neck, larynx, mouth, pharynx, naseo-pharynx, nasal (nose), sinus, and the structural nature of all bone and flesh immediately associated with those areas. These are the bodily organs and areas which largely affect the nature of basic vocal resonation after proper breath has been applied to the vocal chords. Further attainment of resonance development is realized from the intelligent use of the

organs available for tonal resonation. Imbedded in an understanding
of their functions in singing are to be found more misconceptions
and lack of understanding than about almost any other mechanism
involved in the performance of music. Probably there is no subject of vocal study that has more unscientific opinion about the "how"
of achieving intelligent singing than does the subject of resonance development.

Of great importance is the nature of the passage of the vibrations through the various chambers of the throat, mouth, and
head. If historical tradition is important, we are assured by Ce-
rone (1613) that two registers--chest and head--should be recognized.
For some three hundred and fifty years, there has been faith in
registers or at least the recognition of a tonal timbre which may be
identified as chesty and heady. Actually the words chest, middle
(mouth), and head are used to identify tones that seem to resonate
in the chest area, the lower and mid-pharynx area, and the nasal
and forward head area above the nasal pharynx area. Actually, a
clarinet has tones which may be typified by lower, middle, and upper timbres. The instrument, however, will respond with its characteristic qualities, if the embouchure and production do not interfere with the vibratory process. Why? Because we do not alter
the instrument's size, its shape, its bore, and its proportions. The
human instrument is so alterable--this primarily due to psychologi-
cal conditions--that disciplined training is absolutely necessary.

Fillebrown said, "'registers' are a myth," and "head tones,
chest tones, closed tones, open tones," as confined to special parts
of the range of the voice, are distracting distinctions arising from
false education.[1] Another writer stated that, "the different registers of the voice should be regarded as only so many modifications
in the quality of tone, which modifications are inherent in the voice
itself."[2] The writer further emphasized that "these modifications
in quality are not to be brought about by conscious adjustments of
the part employed in making those modifications, as any interfer-
ence with the parts will produce that obstacle to smoothness and
equality in the scale which we commonly call a 'break'." In her
book Lilli Lehmann asked "What is a vocal register?" Her reply

is "A series of tones sung in a certain way, which are produced by
a certain position of the vocal organs--larynx, tongue, and palate.
Every voice includes three registers--chest, middle, and head. But
all are not employed in every class of voice."[3] Sir Morell Mackenzie described a register as a "series of tones of like quality pro-
ducible by a particular adjustment of the vocal cords."[4]

Shakespeare preferred to state that the chest register is a
"series of notes in which the vocal cords are said to vibrate in their
entire length and greatest breadth, and which comprises the lowest
tones of the voice."[5] He continued to say that the medium register
is "sometimes called mixed voice, through its being accompanied,
although in a slighter degree, by some vibration of the chest, as
well as the important sense of vibration of the air in the mouth,
which is usually associated with this register. Occasionally it is
termed by Italian masters falsetto, as being inferior in force to the
grander chest voice. Of course, this has no reference to the English term falsetto. In this somewhat lighter series of notes the vocal cords do not, it is said, vibrate with the same breadth as in
the chest register."[6] Regarding the head register he says, "The
head voice consists of a series of notes not only differing in character from those of the chest and medium registers, but presuma-
bly produced by a different action of the vocal cords."[7]

Sometime around 1855 Manuel Garcia, a singing teacher, developed the laryngoscope. With the aid of this instrument visual
observation of the vocal cords in the action of singing could be made.
In spite of this kind of first-hand observation and the many assump-
tions made about the production of sound, the vocal instructor still
has a lack of definitive knowledge concerning exactly how the mind
functions in the production of tonal resonance and exactly what relationship exists between the mind and vibration, pitch, resonance,
and tonal color.

The great singers of the Golden Age of Bel Canto unquestion-
ably knew less than we know today about the physiology and psychol-
ogy of the singing process. Yet, that era produced some of the
greatest artists--possibly some of the greatest singers of all time.
The distinguished baritone, Sir Charles Santley, related in his book

that "Manuel Garcia is held up as the pioneer of scientific teaching
of singing. He was--but he taught singing not surgery! I was a
pupil of his in 1858 and a friend of his while he lived; and in all
the conversations I had with him I never heard him say a word
about larynx or pharynx, glottis or any other organ used in the production and emission of the voice."[8] Intensive study of the methods
of teaching of the early masters reveals that they attempted to induce those conditions which would produce suppleness and freedom
of the entire singing mechanism. What else insures freedom and
proper functioning of the vocal processes?

Registers

Rogers has said that, "The number of registers varies in
different voices. The soprano and contralto voices of full compass
have five registers, the tenor has three, and the bass and baritone
have two. From a physiological standpoint these registers represent
different adjustments of the vocal cords or ligaments, and also different positions of the larynx itself, which wherein different positions cause a variation in the dimensions of the throat."[9] (She refers to the lower chest, upper chest, throat, mouth, and head.)
Actually her major divisions are chest, mouth, and head. Thus,
through a manner which may be considered unscientific, she, too,
has found three major divisions. These registers might be classified as possessing characteristics of tone quality. Although no one
has been able to discern whether the real difference in registers is
only in the larynx box, the opinion is held that variation in registers should be associated with range and singing range areas.

There is some opinion to support the idea that there is a
lower and upper chest, lower and upper mouth, and a lower and upper head register. Whether there are two, three, five, or more
divisions seems unimportant. Certainly, the well-trained singer is
desirous of possessing a voice which has one uniform tone quality,
which is alike in quality from the bottom to the top of his singing
range.

Suppose that there is a lower and upper range (area) tone
quality that is characteristic of a register. This author takes the

position that there is no absolute point where one register exists
and then ceases to exist.   If there is no such line of demarcation,
then it is impossible to accept the thesis that mutable singing processes exist apart from other registers.   This leads to the conclusion that there is no immutable point beyond or below which certain
type actions exist.   Furthermore, the fact can be posited that the
process within a register and from register to register is a continuous ascending and descending functional act without physical
change.   This theory of non-mutability emphasizes that in singing
from the lower to the upper reaches of a given register (all registers for that matter) there is an ever increasing need for greater
breath energization, greater employment of tonal resonation and
more precise mental conceptions of where the individual is singing
at all times.   Proper breathing is not the only requirement for
achieving great singing.   A consummate understanding of resonance
and physical processes required for producing a good tone is dependent upon all the associative functions that have been discussed.   It
is believed that poor tones in any area of the singing range are the
result of poor associative mental and physical processes.

The Chest Register

        Basic to a discussion on registers should be a systematic
treatment of each register as it is now quite correctly discussed, if
not entirely accepted.   The descriptive use of the words, Chest,
Mouth, and Head then become words to describe areas of resonation.   Their function in singing is discussed in the following pages.
        The lower chest tones are usually more easily produced.
The singer is relaxed and unconsciously he seems to feel that great
care must not accompany the singing of these lower tones.   Too often the singer's mental conceptions are wrong; consequently, the
tone suffers and there is a great unevenness of tonal line.   There
must be developed a union between those tones that are characteris-
tically chest tones and those which often give the impression of being solely developed through mouth resonation.   If there is an indi-
vidualization of concept of tones for the chest area, that would rule
out the concept of dynamic conception from note to note through the

entire singing range. If the reader will refer back to the non-
mutable theory of function in singing from the bottom to the top of
a singing voice, he will more fully understand what is meant here.

    Some Chest Register Observations. The larynx moves some-
what lower in its throat position in the production of low tones.
There are those vocal teachers who believe that this low position
has a definite associative relation with chest resonance in the singing of tones in this lower sequence. This is not to infer a belief
that registers exist--except in so far as their associative qualities
have been attached to a description of the voice when it is producing tone in the lower, middle, and head or upper resonance areas
of the singing range.

    The difficulty with Chest Register (or any Register Concept)
concepts is that when adherred to with tenacity, the singer usually
develops a stiff larynx singing mechanism. Diagram (A) indicates
a bore of tone with uniformity throughout its entire length.

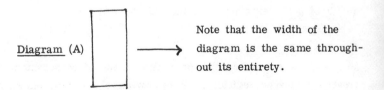

Diagram (A)

Note that the width of the
diagram is the same throughout its entirety.

The uniformity of tone quality should be the same throughout its entire register or singing range. Diagram (B) shows some uniformity of bore (timbre) in the middle of the register (a) and a spread-
forced-overblown tonal bore in its upper and lower limits (b), thereby altering the uniformity of the tone quality.

    Whenever the singer finds that his tone quality follows rather
closely the implications discussed and diagrammed by illustration
(B) in any area (register) of the singing voice, it is quite certain
that nearly all of the characteristics of poor tone production with
which this study is concerned are certain to be present to greater
or lesser degree. A poor singing tone will never possess only one
fault, but rather will manifest many varying degrees of undesirable

tone quality.

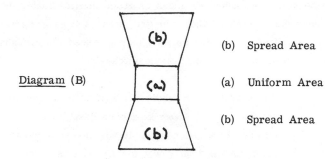

Diagram (B)

(b)   Spread Area

(a)   Uniform Area

(b)   Spread Area

The following exercises will help the choral singer counter-act the commonly found undesirable singing habits that affect the tone quality as suggested by Diagram (B).

Exercises

1. Vocalize, using the darker colored vowels ō and ōō. If these vowels are produced with care, noting the exactness of their true sound, they will aid in induc-ing more uniform tonal bore (timbre).

2. Vocalize, using the vowel ō and ōō as follows:

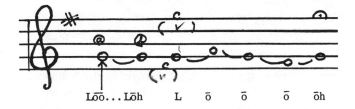

Lōō... Lōh   L   ō   ō   ō   ōh

a) Use Loo to focus resonance forward in the mask of the face; b) Shift from the singing of Loo to Lōh without stopping the tone (be careful to retain the Loh in the same resonance area, as was experienced in the singing of the Loo); c) Take a breath before articulating the Lōh.

The spreading of the bore (timbre) will occur if the singer allows the vowel to change its focus of resonance in singing ascending or descending pitches other than the pitch used as a starting point for vocalization. Likewise, the inexperienced singer usually spreads the tone in singing such scale pitches.

> 3. Concentrate on a circle (O) written on a sheet of paper and placed where it can be easily seen. The purpose of this technique is to prevent mind wandering from the true vowel form. The assumption is that the vowel can be no truer in form than that which is mentally conceived by the singer.

The singer must think of tone production in terms of a vertical rather than a horizontal or spread concept. Bigness must be ruled out because it always induces breathy tone quality, poor intonation, ineffective tonal energization and carrying power, and limits the singer's effective vocal range.

With the aid of the instructor the singer must be taught to find his natural singing voice. Too many singers want to be something other than what they actually can effectively become. The idea of tonal bigness ruins more singing voices than is commonly known. Simplicity of vocal expression is the surest way of arriving at some common sense basis for finding an individual's natural voice. Simplicity and naturalness of vocal expression usually help the singer to eventually become more effective than he at first thinks possible, because such an approach has a definite tendency to induce a natural singing tone. Relaxation must be attained before such a goal is achieved.

The singer is more likely to achieve better tonal uniformity throughout his singing range if he employs the concepts which are implied in the following diagrams:

Diagram (C) Uniformity of Tonal Timbre (Bore)

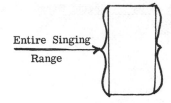

Entire Singing
Range

The singer as well as the auditor
has a right to expect the emanation
of the same tone quality from the
entire singing range of the human
voice as they would from any instrument.

Diagram (D) Potential Tonal Sensation Concept for Entire
Singing Range

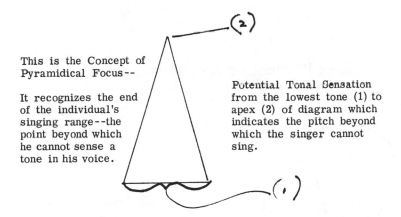

This is the Concept of
Pyramidical Focus--

It recognizes the end
of the individual's
singing range--the
point beyond which
he cannot sense a
tone in his voice.

Potential Tonal Sensation
from the lowest tone (1) to
apex (2) of diagram which
indicates the pitch beyond
which the singer cannot
sing.

If the singer will employ the pyramidical tonal focus concept rather than a uniform or spread concept in singing,
he will more nearly approach a uniformity of tonal quality which the voice is capable of producing with ease
throughout the singing range. A pyramidical tonal concept will help to eliminate tone of undesirable quality.
Good tone is conceived in the mind. The singer must
get his mental concept of tone straightened out before he
can expect to emit desirable tone.

Diagram (E) Potential Tonal Sensation Concept Based on
             Continuous Uniformity of Bore Without Con-
             sideration for Finality of Singing Range

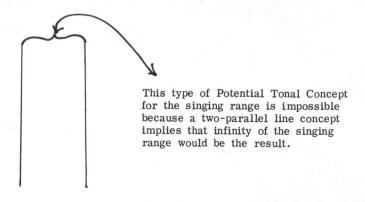

This type of Potential Tonal Concept
for the singing range is impossible
because a two-parallel line concept
implies that infinity of the singing
range would be the result.

Diagram (F) Tonal Concepts Superimposed Upon Uniform
             Bore (Timbre) Concept

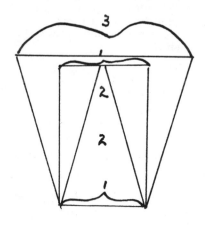

1. Normal Tonal Bore Concept
2. Pyramidical Concept
3. Spread Bore Concept

Diagram (D) is the pyramidical tonal conception which illustrates
the sensation for the focus of a tone which must be adjusted to meet
ascending and descending pitch levels. By employing the pyramidical concept the singer thinks in terms of concentrating his tonal focus and its resultant resonation in relation to the topmost tone of

his singing range. This concept is opposed to the Normal Tonal
Bore Concept, which because of its uniformity does not alter the focus and the resultant need for intensification of energization throughout its entire range.

Diagram (G)
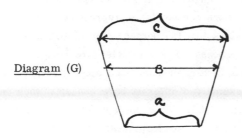

The spread bore concept is certain to insure trouble for the
singer's tone. If it is assumed that point (a) represents the normal
tonal bore (timbre) for a singer, then it can easily be discerned
that any point above it (b) would indicate the degree of diffusion or
tonal spread beyond the natural timbre (bore) of the voice. In other
words, an overblown voice (c) can never be a natural sounding voice.
It is obvious from this discussion that any voice tonally performing
as indicated in Diagram (G) puts a great burden on the voice. Such
a tonal concept if pursued for any length of time by a singer is certain to spell ruin for a potentially good singing voice.

Diagram (H) Spread Beginning Tonal Bore Concept. Let us
invert Diagram (G) and start our tonal attack with a spread beginning tonal bore concept.

Diagram (H)
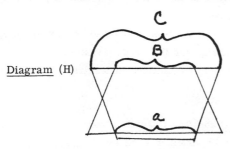

If we were to assume that (b) in Diagram (H) is comparable in bore to (a) in Diagram (G), it would be pertinent to ask if it were possible while singing to decrease the bore concept from (a) to (b) (Diagram (H). This is always impossible because tone production is dependent upon highly intricate intellectual processes that are in continual opposition to any changing situation.   In other words, if a spread beginning tonal bore concept (a) is represented by muscles 274-68-1237, it is obvious that the bore concept of (G) cannot be assumed in the same process, if new muscles are required.   Not alone are ideas entities of a given completed singing action, but as entities they cannot assume two different bore concepts when only one idea has been initiated (a).   Bore concept (b) would have to be reinitiated by the mind as a separate process and therefore the tone would have to be reattacked.

Flexible, Floating, or Resilient Tone.   Tone must be buoyant.   Buoyancy of tone is achieved when the following conditions are met:

1. There is need for adequate breath support.
2. There must be correctly conceived tonal concepts.
3. There must be good head and body singing position.
4. There must be a relaxed tongue which is lying on the floor of the mouth and touching all teeth of the lower jaw.
5. The singer's tone must be adequately focused, energized, and resonated.
6. The lower jaw must not possess any undue muscular tension or rigidity.
7. The musculature of the mask of the face (lips and cheek) must be relaxed.

These seven conditions have all been discussed in this section, but a resumé of them will focus for the reader what is conceived to be the basic mental and physical conditions undergirding tonal resiliency.

The Tenor Voice and The Chest Register.   The tenor voice, especially a lyric tenor, is ineffectual in employing the chest regis-

ter.   Whenever the tenor voice has a resonant chest tone, it will
be that of a robust or heroic tenor.   Robust or heroic tenors (Hel-
den) have a timbre (quality) of voice which is often characteristic
of lyric baritones.   In other words, they have a timbre (quality) of
tone which is meaty and of heavy tonal texture.   The pitches between (c) and (g) in the tenor voice range have some semblance of
a chest register quality (See Illustration).   Not alone do some tenors have difficulty in producing good resonant tones within this area
of their singing range, but they often resort to a forcing or "a bear-
ing down" action of the head in order to achieve more volume (not
quality) in their production.   Such action will produce a hard, strident, and occasionally a guttural tone.

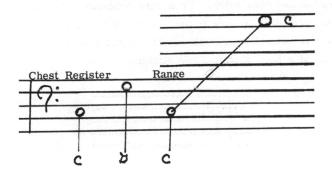

It must be remembered that there is a great variation in
tenor quality as found in choral organizations.   Tenor voices found
in secondary school choirs vary widely due to the use of male and
female singers and because many of the voices are immature.
Church choir tenor sections are usually composed of those whose
voices are tenor in timbre, but are undeveloped and consequently
have the inability to sing above f^2 and g^2 with good tone production.
It is not uncommon to find in the same section, lyric baritones who
are trying to help out the tenor section, or whose voices have been
improperly classified.   These conditions are largely responsible for
the unevenness and poor quality of the tone which often comes from
these choirs.   Whenever an individual strains to sing higher or
louder than he is capable of doing, he is certain to emit forced

tones of poor pitch and quality. Often the natural lyric tenor desires to sing dramatic tenor song repertoire, but forcing of the
tone quality beyond its natural timbre is certain to ruin eventually
the voice of any individual who attempts to alter the naturalness of
his voice.

    The Baritone and Bass Voice and The Chest Register.   The
chest register shows up very prominently in the baritone and bass
voice.   These voices, because of their ability to sing an octave or
more below g, are often capable of producing tones of deep resonant
chest register quality.   The following illustration indicates the tonal
range usually identified as being attributed to the chest register for
the baritone and bass voice.   Upon rare occasion it will be found
that a baritone will be able to sing pitches below g and f (See Illustration), but naturally they will not have tonal bore or timbre characteristic of a bass singing these pitches.

It must be pointed out that the baritone and bass voices of good
range have the probable ranges of:

Baritone

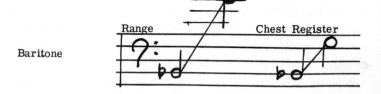

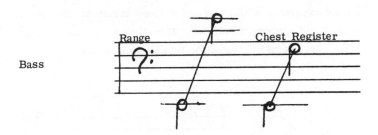

Bass

The Soprano Voice and The Chest Register. For untrained singers the singing and chest register ranges are as follows:

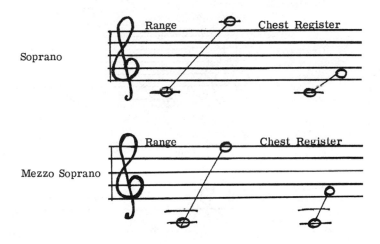

Soprano

Mezzo Soprano

The Contralto Voice and The Chest Register. It is sufficient to indicate but one sub-division of the untrained contralto voice and its chest register range.

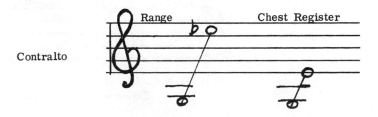

Contralto

The trained soprano--Coloratura-Lyric-Dramatic-Mezzo-- usually experiences chest register tones beginning approximately between f and g above middle c. The following indicated (approximate) chest register areas for these sopranos are:

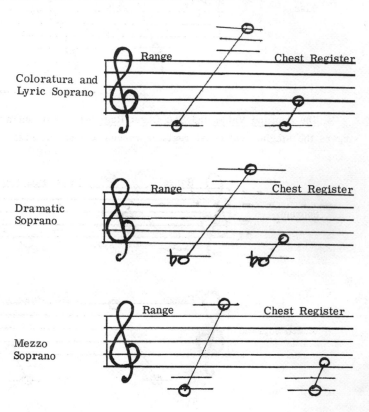

The trained contralto voice ranges should be indicated as follows:

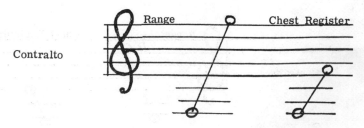

With every voice it is possible to force the singing of the chest register tones much higher than has been indicated, but the continuance of this practice will materially affect the timbre of a voice. The tone will be overblown, of questionable intonation, and lacking in resiliency. Usually the singer's countenance presents evidence of unnecessary tensions. Muscular strain can be observed by noticing tension lines in the lip, cheek, neck and forehead musculature.

The Mouth Register

The mouth register, like the chest register, can be forced up or down from where it is supposed to characterize a certain area of each singer's singing range. Incorrect singing in this register usually causes great tension throughout the musculature under the lower jaw and lips--both upper and lower lip areas. Thus, tonal rigidity and dictional problems will ensue. Naturally there is an associative musculature feeling of tightness.

In all voices, the area encompassing a^1 to e^2

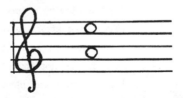

Mouth Register

very nearly includes the entire natural lower and upper limits of the mouth register. The upper limit, e^2, is also the approximate lower limit of the head register. When a singer reaches the e^2 limit of the mouth register, he is, in effect, employing the head register. The lower limit of the mouth register which is usually a^1, may be lowered one-half or one full step further because of the shorter singing range which characterizes certain heavier voices in the contralto, baritone, and bass categories.

In the mouth register the pitches of d^2, e^2, and f^2 are most difficult for tenors, baritones, and basses to produce because they are bridging tones between the mouth and head registers.

These singers must be taught to dovetail or blend the mouth register tones that have been indicated with the head register that is above them. The most critical consideration is getting the head voice fully realized at e^2 and f^2. Many women singers have trouble getting tones of good mouth register quality and resonance at a^1, b^1, and c^2. Light baritones and tenors have difficulty in producing tones of good quality around g^1 and a^1. It is natural to expect most light sopranos and contraltos to experience the same difficulty. Basses have trouble bridging a^1 to d^2 and e^2.

Exercises For Developing The Mouth Register

Preliminary Instructions:

1. Refer to Diagrams C, D, E, F, G, and H (p. 35-37) for retaining proper tonal bore concepts during the act of singing.

2. The ideal tone is first and always correctly conceived mentally before a desirable result can be expected.

3. Before singing a tone or exercise, the singer must give close attention to the many basic vocal techniques which he may have learned. To open the mouth and vocalize is not enough. Always attempt to set up as ideal mental and physical conditions as possible before singing a tone or exercise.

Ex. I

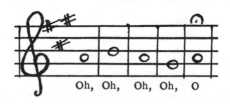

Oh, Oh, Oh, Oh, O

a. It is usually desirable to start with the vowel Ō. The circular concept is conducive to producing the vowel more correctly. The singer should visualize circular-ness if he is to produce well-rounded Ō tones.

b. The singer should always think of verticalness in relation to the flow of the tonal sound that is passing
through his body. This idea is an aid to him in keeping his concept of Ō (Ōhness) within a controllable
concept which will permit greater tonal energization.
His Ō is to be produced within this vertical form he
conceives, thereby permitting greater tonal energization.

Ex. II

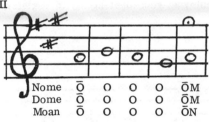

Nome	Ō	O	O	O	ŌM
Dome	Ō	O	O	O	ŌM
Moan	Ō	O	O	O	ŌN

Sing Exercises
Chromatically Up
and Down the
Scale.

a. Some singers respond more readily if the vowel Ō is
imbedded in a consonant prefixed to a one syllable
word. The consonant articulation is often helpful in
stressing the vowel which is the tonal core and purveyor of the tone within the word.

b. Be certain that the tonal attack is precise and listen
for any undue amount of breathiness in the tone.
(See section on Tonal Breathiness)

Ex. III

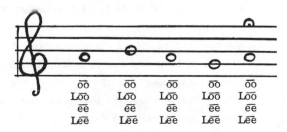

o͞o	o͞o	o͞o	o͞o	o͞o
Lo͞o	Lo͞o	Lo͞o	Lo͞o	Lo͞o
e͞e	e͞e	e͞e	e͞e	e͞e
Le͞e	Le͞e	Le͞e	Le͞e	Le͞e

a. Start with a forward resonating vowel such as o͞o or
   e͞e. Usually these two vowels give the singer considerable resonation in the mask of the face. He
   gets a feeling of the forward tonal sensation (position)
   which is very often absent in the singing of tones in
   the mouth resonance.

b. After attaining a good sounding o͞o or e͞e, with strong
   facial (mask of the face) resonation, it is then suggested that the vowels be joined with the more open
   vowel Ō. Exercise IV has proved extremely helpful
   in achieving good opulent mouth register tone for
   singers.

Ex. IV

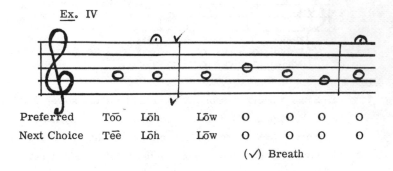

| Preferred | To͞o | Lōh | Lōw | O | O | O | O |
| Next Choice | Te͞e | Lōh | Lōw | O | O | O | O |

(✓) Breath

a. Start with To͞o (Similar to Arabic 2) for better beginning tonal articulation.

b. Without stopping tone try to retain forward sensation
   (position) of vowel o͞o and continue tonal sustainment
   through to singing vowel Ōh. The objective is to produce Ōh with the same forward sensation as experienced in the singing of the vowel o͞o.

c. After sustaining the Ōh, take a breath and rearticu-
   late the syllable and complete the exercise as indicated in Exercise IV. Be sure when rearticulating
   the Ōh, that the forward tonal sensation does not
   change. The great objective is not to change the uniformity of the tonal resonation from one pitch to an-

other.

Naturally, results are often slow and perseverance is essential. Employing these exercises intelligently over a period of time
is certain to produce good mouth resonance and tone quality.

Ex. V After the singer has been able to sing Exercises I-
IV with a measure of success, he should attempt
singing the following:

Loh, Loh, Loh, Loh, Loh, Loh, Loh, Loh, Loh, Loh, etc.

a. Great care must be exercised in the singing of the
ascending scale to see that no spread or loss of tonal resonation occurs. Reader is again referred to
Diagrams C-H (p. 35-37).

Ex. VI After practicing Exercise V the singer may increase
its range to:

Loh, Loh, Loh, Loh, Loh, Loh, Loh, Loh, Loh, etc.
Move Up and Down Scale

Thus far we have employed vowels ōo, ēe, and ō. When
much practice has been exercised in singing Exercises I-VI, the
singer should be ready for singing vowel äh. The singing of äh
has been deferred because its form is conducive to the singing of a
shallow, horizontally conceived, vowel form rather than a vertically
induced tonal sensation. In order to retain what has already been
gained, the following exercise is conducive toward making the tran-
sition from vowel ō to vowel äh effectual for retaining good mouth

resonance. Naturally, the vowel ō concept must be basically good--
otherwise vowel ăh cannot be good.

Ex. VII

Nōh, Năh,   Nōh, Năh,   Nōh, Năh,   Nōh, Năh, Nōh, etc.
Năh, Nōh,   Năh, Nōh,   Năh, Nōh,   Năh, Nōh, Năh, etc.

        After success has been achieved in singing the exer-
cise with the syllable arrangement we have just indicated,
it is recommended that their singing order should be altered.
        Another method for retaining the fidelity of the Ō
form can be achieved by using Exercise VIII.

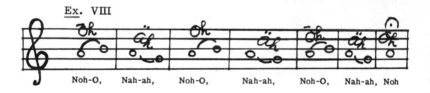

Ex. VIII

    Noh-O,   Nah-ah,   Noh-O,   Nah-ah,   Noh-O,   Nah-ah, Noh

        The following exercise can be used equally well:

Ex. IX

    Nōh-Ōh,   Năh-ăh,   Nōh-Ōh,   Năh-ăh,   Nōh-Ōh,   Năh.
    Move Up and Down Scale

Again it is possible to alternate the Nōh-Ōh beginning
syllable by starting with Näh-Äh. Refer to <u>Exercise</u> VII

The Head Register

Great emphasis has been placed upon the proper development
of tonal timbre within the chest and mouth registers. Just as great
care must be exercised in the development of the head register.
The exercises that have been suggested for the proper development
of the chest and mouth register are likewise applicable for the development of the head register. The critical consideration now is
to dovetail the mouth and head registers.

<u>Dovetailing Registers</u>. It must be understood that no regis-
ter is complete unto itself with the same timbre (quality) remaining
distinct for a given area of the singing voice (mouth register) and
then becomes sharply contrasted when employed for another area of
the singing range. Registers are referred to as having characteristics of chest, mouth, and head tone quality, but that does not signi-
fy different vocal chord or physical action in the throat. It might
be better to talk of chest, mouth, and head resonation, rather than
registers, but the latter term has been chosen because of its tradi-
tional use in attempting to describe the tonal sound identified throughout a vocalist's singing range. A singer's voice should be a continuous succession of tones which are alike in timbre from his lowest
to his highest singing tone. The word register--divided into three
categories for the entire singing range--connotes only timbre characteristics.

The mouth register as it approaches the head register must
become a blending of lower head tone (timbre) and the upper timbre
of the mouth register which must have some elements of head voice
timbre. The teacher of singing and the choral director must recognize the gradualness of this action as the singer sings through his
mouth register into his head register.

If the mouth register were represented by <u>Diagram</u> (a) and
the head register by <u>Diagram</u> (b),

Diagram (a)   Diagram (b)

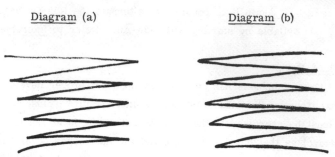

it can be easily seen that the two registers or tonal timbres could not possibly mesh unless they were brought together--Diagram (c).

Diagram (c)

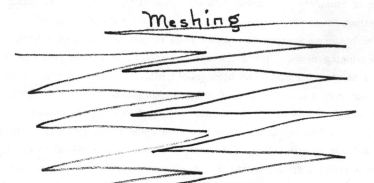

Bringing some head voice (timbre) down to be fused with the mouth register will make for better overall tonal timbre alignment between the two registers. Some special exercises are now offered to help the singer bring about the meshing of the mouth and head registers. It is important to use vocal syllables that will give good head resonation.

Exercises

YuM,   YuM,   YuM,   YuM,   YuM,   YuM,   YuM, etc.
YoM,   YoM,   YoM,   YoM,   YoM,   YoM,   YoM, etc.

It is imperative that the singer strongly resonate
the M at the end of each word (syllable), and hold the
third syllable for a period of time longer than the other
two syllables of the exercise in order to stress the third
syllable's M resonation.

It is always better to start this exercise on the higher pitched tone because the singer gains confidence if he
successfully produces the first note. Singing up the
scale (in any exercise) is always conducive to tensions.

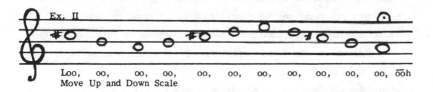

Loo,   oo,   oo,   oo,   oo,   oo,   oo,   oo,   oo,   oo,   oo,   ōoh
Move Up and Down Scale

The singer in using Exercise II, should sing the exercise very lightly, with as much sensation of headiness
as it is possible to experience. We have started the exercise a third above the regular beginning note in a sequence of five tones in order to give the singer a feeling
of confidence which he should derive from singing successfully the higher beginning note in this exercise. The
syllable lōo should possess a strong feeling of being focused or energized through the nose.

Generally speaking, the head register can be brought down to

(a^1) in most voices.   As a matter of fact, it can be forced down lower, but its results are not always satisfying if employed by the inexperienced singer.   Whenever forcing occurs in producing a sing- ing tone the results may be deleterious to good tone production and the timbre of the singer's voice.

The beginning of the head voice is e^2, for all singers. Nearly all baritones, tenors, and mezzo-sopranos should sing e^2 in the head (resonance) register.   The absolute bridging tone for many of the voices in these three categories is e-flat^2.   It is believed that for eighty to ninety percent of the sopranos, e^2 should be in the head register and the remainder of their classification should use this register when singing f^2.   If this is not done, the singer will force his mouth register beyond natural limits with the result the tone will become hard, strident, and unmusical.

If what we have said is reasonably true, then the f^2 is too late to prepare for singing with good tonal alignment between the mouth and head register.   Therefore, effective head tone (register) study can never be started at the point where the mouth register ends and the head register begins.   There must be a study of head register preparation and tonal sensation three or four tones prior to a full use of the head register.   By studying where the first tone of the head register begins, or for that matter where any register be- gins, the artificiality of registers becomes more apparent.   Vocal instruction along this approach to the development of uniformity of tonal timbre very often results in the appearance of unrelated and differentiated tone quality in a singer's voice.

It has already indicated that a full major third must be care- fully prepared prior to the singing for the first head tone in order to make the necessary timbre adjustment (meshing) between the mouth and the head register.   There is always a need for a proper mental conception of tone before it can be intelligently produced.

Generally speaking it may be said that for most voices, c^2 is the preparatory point for proper head register development; e-flat^2 is the bridging tone, and e^2 and f^2 are the pitches where tones must be produced fully in the head register by medium and high pitched voices.   We would like to emphasize again that in every

voice every tone needs proper breath support; there must be accu-
rate tonal conception; and there must be a tonal bore concept in
keeping with needs of the tone, if each tone is to be properly conceived in relation to all other pitches throughout all registers of the
singer's voice. Within the entire singing range every tone needs
its own individualized conception.

Notes

1. Thomas Fillebrown Resonance in Singing and Speaking, p.5.

2. Clara Kathleen Rogers The Philosophy of Singing, p.90.

3. Lilli Lehman How to Sing, p.133.

4. Sir Morell Mackenzie The Hygiene of the Vocal Organs.

5. William Shakespeare The Art of Singing, Part I, p.36.

6. Ibid., p.38.

7. Ibid., p.41.

8. Fillebrown op. cit., p.3.

9. Rogers op. cit., p.90-91.

Chapter III

Tone Production and Resonance Development

Imbedded in registers is our focus upon tone quality or timbre in reference to the entire singing range of any voice. For centuries the terms chest, mouth, and head voice have been used to
identify singing tone register qualities. Resonance is the word commonly used to identify the degree of tonal timbre reinforcement (intensity) possessed by an individual's chest, mouth, or head voice
quality. Fillebrown emphasized the fact that "resonance determines
the quality and carrying power of every tone, and is therefore the
most important element in the study and training of the voice."[1]

Much resonance study--its development and employment
throughout the range of a singer's voice--is important to a proper
understanding of how to apply breath and maintain an ever present
control and support while singing. The opinion is held that the quality of tone is dependent upon the quality of the tonal concept. Proper concepts have much to do with attaining good tonal resonance.
Lamperti said that "There is no doubt that the greater part of the
difficulties encountered at a change of register, as well as the uneven tones within one and the same register, may be traced to faulty
breathing."[2] Keep in mind that adequacy of breath and proper tonal
balance (support) are likewise dependent upon excellent chord and
vibratory processes.

Important Considerations in Resonance Development

1. Any voice that produces its tones peculiarly to a single
register (chest, mouth, head) will, if allowed to continue, bring
about doom for the quality of that voice. Eventually there will develop a natural break in the quality of the individual's singing voice.
The instrument will sound differently in different pitch areas. It is

54

a common observation that any continuance or expansion of such a falsely produced voice will result in detrimental effects upon the musculature of the singer's throat.

2. Any voice that does not have an even alignment of tone throughout its singing range is usually pitted with areas of weak and strong tones. In other words there has not been uniformity of resonance and tonal development. An intelligent study of resonance is certain to assure any voice greater flexibility, tonal uniformity, and singing effectiveness.

3. Most singers' voices lack tonal uniformity and it can be easily detected. The objective of this whole book is to aid students in achieving good tone production.

4. Singers have difficulty because they unduly force their voices and thus impede the natural characteristics of their tone quality. In singing a tone, the singer must be certain that the tones immediately above and those below it must be conceived in correct relation to the sung tone. Thus, a larynx action for d^1 must not also be held to the line for e^1. Without consideration for the changing resonance which has been indicated, musculature becomes hardened and the quality of the tone suffers.

5. In keeping with the significance of point 4, breath support must be continually undergirding each note, because if the breath is at any time inadequate, the throat must assume the burden of singing and tension occurs. Every note in every scale must possess a sensitivity or "feelingness" that implies that it has a specific resonance concept. If this is lost, resonance for each tone does not have the individuality which it can and should achieve.

6. There must always be an uninterrupted flow of tone while singing the vowel forms--a constancy of breath support will certainly aid the possibility of resonating vowel forms. Wherever its sensation is felt (head), palate (mouth), or lower mouth (chest), there must always be a balance between the breath and throat, and the concept of the vowel form must be constant.

7. It is well established that vibrations ascend into the resonating cavities. Because this is true, great study must be made of the part played by the resonating cavities in providing their optimum

of resonation for the vibrations which they will entertain. The singer must learn to control his tonal resonations. He must learn to
become sensitive to the minutest differentiations of resonation that
are possible within a tone and from tone to tone. Resonation discrimination becomes a major task for both teacher and pupil.

8. The use of the falsetto may play an important part in the
development of the upper (head register) voice for men; it is rarely
if ever used in training women's voices.

9. Breath pressure (resistance) against the chest seemingly
helps in the control of tonal emission and often results in the production of good tonal resonance. The distribution of pressure--re-
sistance must be felt across the front of the chest--is important to
get a distribution of this feeling throughout the front (anterior) chest
area.

10. Because the tongue is immediately above the larynx, it
is very important that it be given close attention. If it is driven
down the throat, it will interfere with the resonance possibilities in
those resonating chambers which lie directly above the opening of
the throat in the mouth area. The tongue must touch the gum of the
front lower teeth. The tongue must not be sucked or drawn back into the throat. Actually, it is desirable to have as great a mouth
area resonating space as possible. There is some evidence to indicate that the height of the tongue in the posterior portion of the
mouth must follow the positions assumed by the larynx while there
is singing. There must never be a stiff larynx.

11. In mouth register (palatal resonance singing) the palate
plays a tremendous role in the focus of tone. Some authorities believe that it should appear that the tones are actually focused in the
palatal area. Seemingly the breath is focused upon the palate or the
point of tonal attack. Thus, the palate becomes a point of resistance.

Developing Inherent Resonances

The object is to develop a similarity instead of dissimilarity
of tone quality. Whether the idea of registers is used or not, the
choral director and singer must recognize that beauty of tonal timbre

cannot be attained unless the study of tone quality and voice (scale) equalization becomes the major objective of vocal study. All voices inherently possess resonance, but therein lies the challenge: how to train singers to sing with beautiful vocal resonation. The following provocative considerations and suggestions should prove helpful in dealing with the problem of tonal timbre.

1. Resonance and how it is to be employed must be made for every tone in the singer's vocal range. We believe this statement to be technically sound, possible, and when achieved, satisfying to the singer.

2. Vowel resonation will greatly improve if the individual will sense vowels in an aspirated manner. Try the following exercise.

a) Say (sense) ā, ē, ō, ōō breathily, but do not intone them. Allow the mouth, lips, and tongue positions to comply with the actions which are initiated by the vowels without attempting to force with lip-jaw movements undue actions that may impair the desired natural formations. It is desired that any lip-jaw movements which may have been preconceived for making vowels rather than allowing the mind to dictate natural mouth formations should be eliminated if at all possible.

b) While sensing the vowels try to discern the nature of the mouth and tongue positions. Alternate the exercise under (a) with the following: ā, ōō, ē, ō. Attempt many other combinations in order to discern the contrasting tongue and mouth positions.

c) Sometimes it is wise to start vocalizing by articulating (sensing) the various vowels, either singly or in groups, and then intone the various vowel forms, but start them either singly, or sequentially as follows:

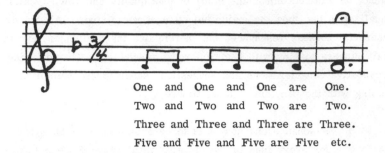

One and One and One are One.
Two and Two and Two are Two.
Three and Three and Three are Three.
Five and Five and Five are Five etc.

This simplified method is recommended for vocalizing vowels. The exercise is a great aid for induc-
ing simplicity and relaxation for the inexperienced
singer. Very often vocalizes become more pro-
found in their content than is needed. Simplicity of
approach to the problem of finding natural lip,
tongue, and mouth formations is a major objective
in attempting to attain good vowel formations and
tone production.

3. When intoning vowels the choral director and singer
should be careful that not more breath is used in their
production than is needed. Too often the singing tone is
carrying an excess amount of breath. Check tone with
this exercise:

a) Light a match and hold the burning flame five inches
from the open mouth. Note how the flame is react-
ing while singing. If the flame unduly flickers at
this distance the singer can be assured that his tone
is breathy. Very frequently when the singer intones
a sound, the flame will be immediately extinguished.
It is possible to hold a flame one inch from the
mouth without its flickering. This device will help
the choral director and teacher of singing convince
singers that they have a tone which is too breathy.

b) It is highly desirable to have tones produced by a
   <u>neat</u> application of breath pressure on any vowel or
   syllable at a given pitch with correct intensity.
   Every tone's pitch requires the correct number of
   double vibrations per second (DVs) in keeping with
   the dynamics of its functional demands. Every tone
   needs the correct amount of breath, intensity of
   energization, and resonation.

   Tonal attack can be greatly improved and its
   breathiness largely eliminated through the observance of the following practices:

   1) Practice slowly listening to the sound of the
   tones that are produced. Be certain that the tonal
   attack is precise. Think cleancut tonal attacks because they are the disciplines out of which better
   tone quality is produced. A singer must learn to
   attune his ear to the sound of his voice.

   2) Use a cleancut staccato attack as suggested
   in the following exercise:

Hah, Hah, Hah, Hah,   Hah
Hoh, Hoh, Hoh, Hoh,   Hoh.

Move up and down the scale--Use only in the comfortable singing range of the voice.

4. Every degree of vowel formation and deviation from the
   purity of its true form is certain to change the nature of
   its resonation. Every change in shading is the result of
   musculature adjustments initiated by the mind. Usually
   when an individual is asked to sing a vowel on a high
   pitched note and again on a pitch an octave below it, there

is a noticeable change in the sound of that vowel. It is the job of the choral director to train the singer to be consistent in the production of all vowel forms.

5. Most singers produce vowel sounds in the flat of the mouth (mouth register). Use dark vowels (ōh, ōō) for vocalizing those singers who habitually speak or sing in the flat of the mouth (mouth register). Use bright vowels (ēh, ěh, ǎh) for those who use a dark lugubrious speaking or singing tone quality.

6. Although good resonance is naturally inherent to the singing voice, very few individuals know how to obtain even its minimum effectiveness for singing. For resonance development it is helpful to use ōō, because this vowel gives the singer a depth of tonal sensation and a forward focus for its resonation.

7. In the development of resonance, all vowels should have the forward resonant sensation of the ōō as in two. Any change in this forward resonance sensation will adversely affect the resonant quality of any tone. Usually as the singer ascends the scale, there is a movement in resonance sensation (position) from the front to the back of the mouth. This is due to the lack of mental and physical energization on the quality of tonal timbre that is to be achieved by the singer. This constant vitiation of tonal resonation and energization is largely due to the fact that the beginning singer does not know how to achieve a uniform resonant singing tonal scale throughout his singing range.

8. A better understanding of the text will automatically color emotions and they, in turn, will be reflected in tone quality. Live the text. As excitation activates bodily action, it is certain that greater individual absorption of the vocal text will motivate mental conception and physical drive in the total singing process.

9. The nature of the resonating chamber determines to a considerable extent tonal resonance. All organs or areas

such as the teeth, jaw, tongue, palate, naseo-pharynx chamber--any alterable organ or cavity is certain to make alterations in the resonating chamber and thus affect tonal timbre. It cannot be emphasized too often what an important role the right type of thinking plays in the development of tonal resonance.

Resonance Exercises for Effective Inducement of Tone

Exercise I

Put two fingers more than half-way into the mouth. Say: Nōh, Näh, Nōh. Note the dampered resonances. Resonance is definitely affected by alteration of the resonating chambers.

Exercise II

Sing on a comfortable singing pitch, Tōō, Lōh, Tōō. Note the changed resonation position (sensation) in the head and mouth. The sensation may be different, but there should never be a constant fluctuation in the utilization of all the cavities for tonal resonation. Use tōō, to get form and positional feeling before singing Lōh. Note carefully whether or not there has been a shift in the amount of the forward resonation which characterized the singing of Lōō. The singer should feel this forward resonation for the singing of all vowels.

Exercise III

After the singing of Tōō has been correctly established, sing on a given pitch, Nōme, Dōme, Lōam, or Hōme. Be certain that the voiced consonants N or M are given good resonance sustainment. Be sure that in sustaining the resonation of the N or M that the sensation be felt in the same area as for Tōō.

Exercise IV

Try tasting the vowel Ōh, by first saying and then singing
YO<u>M</u>. After this exercise has been tried, then attempt the
singing of YU<u>M</u>, but be sure that there is complete relaxation
of the musculature of the throat, mouth, and face; emphasize
the sustainment of the <u>M</u> at the end of the syllable. Try
this exercise in the middle lower, middle, and especially in
the bridging area of the mouth-head region (see section de-
scribing these range areas) of the male and female voice
ranges. In the singing of these exercises the singer should
simulate the action of tasting something, such as food, and
by both saying and singing YOM. If there is any twang or
buzz, open the nostrils and sing with an attitude of inspira-
tion or elevation of both mental and physical well-being.

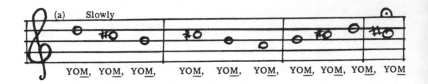

Variation of above Exercise (a)

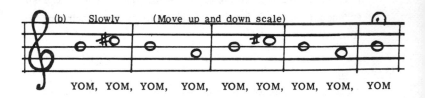

Variation of Exercise (b)

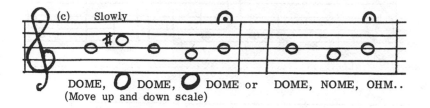

DOME, DOME, DOME or DOME, NOME, OHM..
(Move up and down scale)

Exercise V

Practice the following exercises employing the vowels, o͞o,
e͞, and o͞ respectively.

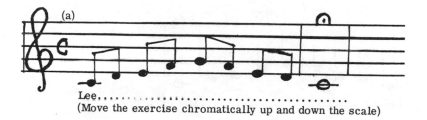

Lee.......................................
(Move the exercise chromatically up and down the scale)

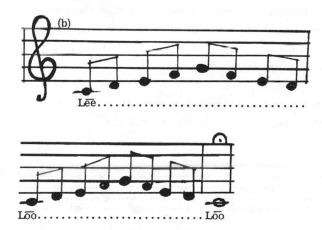

Le͞e...............................

Lo͞o....................... Lo͞o

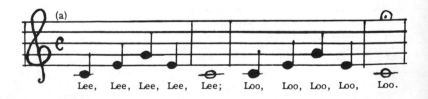

Lēē..............................Lōō..............

Lōō...........Lōh...................................

Lēē or Lōō.....................Lēē or Lōō

The singer should be very careful to end each exercise with
as correct tongue and mouth position as it is possible for
him to establish.   The purpose of the exercise is to induce
and maintain superior tonal resonance.

After the singer has succeeded in correctly singing the fore-
going exercises, he is ready for the following:

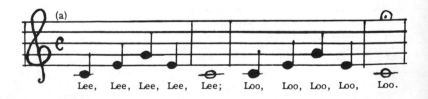

Lee,   Lee,   Lee,   Lee,   Lee;   Loo,   Loo, Loo, Loo,   Loo.

Nee, Nee, Nee, Nee, Nee;   Noo, Noo, Noo, Noo,   Noo.

Nee-Noo, Nee-Noo, Nee-Noo, Nee-Noo, Nee-Noo; etc.

Nee-Noo-Noh, Nee-Noo-Noh, Nee-Noo-Noh, Nee-Noo-Noh, etc.

Noh, Noh, Noh, Noh, Noh.

All exercises should be started slowly. In the singing of
Exercise V, (a-e), be sure that the bore or timbre of the
tone does not spread as the singer ascends and descends the
step intervals. In all of these suggested exercises the vowel
in the end syllable should be sustained with great care. The
choral director and singer should begin the exercises at a

pitch level that is suitable to the individual's voice range.
In the early study of singing, it is often true that the singer
may have but a limited singing range. The exercises should
be pitched with this consideration in mind. Although we have
indicated but one measure exercises, the individual can repeat the measures as many times as seems feasible.

Exercise VI

Word elisions which are embodied in word phrases are very
good for developing strong tonal resonation. The three word
phrase idea can be used for this purpose. The following
phrases serve excellently in the development of resonation.

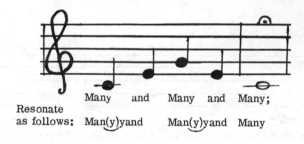

Many   and   Many   and   Many;

Resonate
as follows: Man(y)yand   Man(y)yand   Many

Home   and   Home   and   Home

Hom mand   Hom mand   Home

It is recommended that the singer elide one syllable with the
sequential syllable in such a manner that the voiced consonants which are indicated bring out the utmost in resonation.

Factors Affecting Tone Production and Intonation

Good tonal pitch (intonation) is striven for by all performing musicians. It is dependent upon many mental and physical factors. An individual's aural acuity, emotional temperament, and general physical health are the great determinants in the ability of the singer to sing with good pitch fidelity. It also is a well-known fact that many singers can improve their intonation by learning how to sing tones of good quality if they have the necessary emotional fire to elevate the psycho-physical being into a good rapport for effective singing. The following are some of those factors that influence tonal timbre and intonation.

1. Diffused Tonal Timbre Conceptions. Such a situation occurs when the singer overblows his natural voice out of all proportion to its inherent character. The individual's mental concept of his tone is one of bigness. The singer has an expanded feeling in the posterior region of the throat. The tone is often very breathy and the pitch becomes false or uncertain. Naturally, this brings about a ruination of pure vowel forms.

2. Inadequate Breath Support (Incorrect Breathing). If the vocal cords are being starved of the breath needed for the vibratory demands of a given pitch, then the tone will be of poor intonation. If the singer's mental concept is such that it induces a flaccid physical approach to tonal delivery-- usually resulting in a blowing out of the tone--then the pitch will be falsified. The latter condition will result in a tone that is hooty and the singer's voice will be ineffectual.

If the individual is using incorrect breathing, he will sing with strictured throat action resulting in an improper balance between the breath and the vocal cords. Such a condition will cause a strident tone and it will be falsified in intonation. There must always be a one-to-one relationship of balance between breath and vocal cord action. The breath is the stream of life upon which the tone depends for its existence.

We must mention that an over supply of breath is certain to affect the pitch of a tone. If a pitch requires 256 DVs per second and the individual is applying pressure or breath support equivalent to 476 DVs, yet mentally holding to the concept of 256, it is obvious that intonation and resulting timbre will be overblown in its bigness and its pitch sharpened or both.

In instrumental playing, with the instrument core firm and unchanging, it can be easily discerned that if there is any overblowing of tonal timbre, it is not the result of spreading the instrument's structural form. Spreading of a singer's tonal bore (timbre) is likely to happen anywhere in the entire range of his voice. In addition, the spreading of tone is undoubtedly easier to control in the middle voice than it is in the extreme upper and lower singing range. Every time a singer produces a tone he must refashion his instrument (voice) in order to produce sound. It is this constant remaking of his instrument that requires such refined expression of his mental and physical singing disciplines.

3. <u>Incorrect Voice-Type Classification (Diagnosis)</u>. Many incorrect voice-type diagnoses (classifications) are made when voice testing takes place. Frequently singers are classified correctly as to soprano, alto, tenor, or bass, but they are incapable of singing the vocal range which is expected of them because of the music which is selected for them to sing. Too often singers are required to sing voice parts and song literature for which they have neither the vocal training, musicianship, nor vocal equipment to adequately perform. There is a tremendous difference, for example, between coloratura and dramatic soprano voices. If the tessitura (lie of the melodic line), range, or style (lyric or dramatic) are not in keeping with their mental and physical equipment, the development of their voice may be retarded and functionally impaired.

In singing groups there frequently may be found tenors who are in reality high baritones; sopranos (untrained) who,

though they have short-ranged voices, should be singing on
the alto part; there are baritones who are singing low bass
and do not have the vocal range to do so.   There are many
high school girl alto singers who are actually sopranos, but
because of their good music reading ability are often called
upon to sing the alto part.   It is possible to find many church
choir singers who are improperly classified vocally.   Usually
church choirs sing music arranged for soprano, alto, tenor,
and bass.   There are countless sopranos in church choirs
who are unable to sing with good quality and intonation the
pitches indicated in the following excerpt.   Likewise, it would

Example I

*"Lead us, O Father." (Rockville Centre, L.I., New York; Belwin,
Inc., Octavo 1230, Copyright 1952).   Used by permission of the
publishers, Belwin, Inc., New York, N.Y.

be the exception to find all the sopranos in such a choir producing with clarity and good intonation, a piano tone on A-flat,
as required for the syllable ther (measure 2, Example I).

Example II

*"Let us praise God together on our knees." (Rockville Centre, L.I.,
New York: Belwin, Octavo 1229, Copyright 1952). Used by permission of the publishers, Belwin, Inc., New York, N.Y.

The director should diplomatically indicate those who are to
sing the pitches in the phrase, "lead us, O Father, in the
paths of peace." (Example I.)

Not higher, but a more taxing vocal tessitura, is the
next illustration, "Let us praise God together on our knees"
(Example II.) The help in this phrase is that the ff nature
of the passage _may_ assist the singers in holding intonation.
It would be difficult if the passages were marked pp. Sometimes when the singer is more energized he _may_ sing with
better intonation.

Example III   *

*Rob Roy Perry   "The Strife Is O'er." (Rockville Centre, L.I.,
New York: Belwin, Octavo 1057, Copyright 1952.) Used by permission of the publishers, Belwin, Inc., New York.

The director must be careful to select and classify the
voices correctly and choose music they will be able to sing.

Take the SATB arrangement of "The Strife Is O'er."
(Example III.) Upon three occasions it requires the tenors
to reproduce the following four measures. For a choir with
limited vocal material, the director should evaluate his tenors before selecting this anthem. If alternate notes are sung
the brilliance of the passage would be lost.

It is always detrimental to the timbre of a voice to sing
pitches for which it is not naturally equipped to produce.

If a choir desires to sing four-part music, yet the basses
are primarily first basses (baritones), it would then be un-
wise to choose the following anthem in which the bass part

Example IV

*"Lead Me Lord." (Rockville Centre, L.I., New York: Belwin,
Octavo 1114, Copyright 1952). Used by permission of the publishers, Belwin, Inc., New York, N.Y.

really requires the resonance of good second basses. Nor
would the conglomeration of basses found in many choirs have

the ability to sing resonant tones in the tessitura of the
following excerpt from the same anthem.   There are certain
to be inacurrately sung chords.

Example V

He must think of the midpoint of the best quality of tone of
which each voice section is capable of singing.   A bass part
which presents a good singing range and is quite satisfactory
is in the chorus "With Verdure Clad, " from Haydn's oratorio,
The Creation.   The "Hallelujah Chorus, " from the Messiah,
by Handel, is also well adapted to the basses found in a general chorus.

Example VI is an excellent illustration containing many
of the tessitura problems which we just discussed.   The sopranos and tenors have a high sustained tonal line with much
out of signature notation.

Example VI

*"Raise the glorious." (Rockville Centre, L.I., New York: Belwin,
Octavo 1231, Copyright 1952). Used by permission of the publishers, Belwin, Inc., New York, N.Y.

Keep in mind that lie of the notation in the vocal line is as
important a consideration as is the highest or lowest pitch in
any given part.

In voice testing a determination should be made of that
portion of the singer's range which will produce the best tone
quality. Being able to produce a forced tone on g^2 is different from singing a freely produced tone on e^2. Try to
determine what are the best tones and the extremes of that
range which will produce good intonation. Too often people
in choral groups are encouraged to sing pitches which are not
even in the voice. Duplication of error will not result in
correct musical performance.

Frequently it is possible to make the following adjustments
in assigning voice parts. If the voice is a coloratura or lyric

soprano, it should be assigned to the first soprano part.
The heavier quality voices, such as the dramatic sopranos,
could be assigned to second soprano. Heavier voices do
not have the same vibrancy that the former possess. Those
choral sopranos, as many of them are frequently called,
should be able to sing a^2, or else they will cause the director much trouble, unless his selection of music is of more
limited vocal range requirements. Almost all mezzo-sopranos
should be placed on the alto part in SATB arrangements.

Among those individuals who are singing the alto part
will be found a wide variety of voices. Probably less vocal
harm can be done on this part than on any of the other three
parts. Obviously, the altos must sing in tune, but if the
music is wisely selected, the vocal range requirements can
be limited. Generally speaking the "graveyard" of female
voices is in the alto section. In church choirs the short
ranged sopranos, mezzo-sopranos, and all female voices of
limited range may be assigned to the alto section. Frequently they are assigned to this section in order to strengthen
the inside harmonic part.

The tenors are usually few in numbers. The majority
of choral arrangements for SATB requires them to sing g^1.
Quite often it will be found that there are many short ranged
tenors singing in the tenor section. Upon further examination,
a discriminative director's ear will reveal that many of them
are light or lyric baritones. Keep in mind that such voices
are capable of singing as high as the voice range we have indicated here for the tenors. Unfortunately, however, the
heavier tessitura will tire more quickly than the high baritones on the tenor part, and it is certain to cause them to
sing flat in high sustained tessitura singing. If the director
needs to use light baritones on the tenor part (church choirs),
he should consider using them on second tenor in six and
eight part choral arrangements. Remember that a heavy vibrating voice quality on high notes is certain to have eventual
intonational troubles.

With regard to the basses, it is wise to have the light
or high baritones sing first bass, and the deeper and thicker
quality voices assigned to the lower or second bass part. If
the second or lower basses have difficulty in singing a unison
bass part (SATB), indicate to them just what notes they should
sing.

In testing a voice the important consideration is to find
the midpoint of the individual's best singing range and then
determine the extent of the best singing tones above and below that central point.

4. <u>Aural Acuity and Pitch Discrimination</u>. It is important that the singer have a musical ear--one that has a high
degree of aural acuity. If one ear can hear only in the area
of 5,000 DVs per second (decibles) and another at 15,000, it
is patent that such variations in aural acuity are reflected in
the ability to hear and reproduce tones of good intonation.
The choral director and singer must ever be cognizant of the
fact that aural acuity is the key to all successful musical
learning and performance. Without a good ear musicianship
is certain to flounder. Every good choral director must constantly seek out in everyone of his singers the utmost in
their ability to sing with good intonation.

Tone production is very often poor, because the choral
director's ear is not properly disciplined to discern pitch
variations with minute acuteness. The study of the anatomy
of the ear, important as it may be, will not resolve intonation and tone production problems. It is the trained, experienced, and patient ear that will aid singers in obtaining optimum aural discrimination. Tone will be no better than the
ear's ability to discriminate changing tonal conditions. This
is the reason for the importance of having an excellent vocal
teacher from the very first lesson. The teacher must be an
intuitive and discriminative person. Every voice is different
because every mind is different. A person sings with his
mind as well as with his body.

What can be done to secure good intonation (aural acuity) is the great question. Briefly, it may be said that if the choral director will carefully carry out the suggestions in this book, he is certain to improve the pitch of any choral organization. Specifically, pitch will be determined by the individual composite acuity discrimination of those he is training. The more meticulous he is in selecting singers for their musicianship, the more likely he is to get a better result, pitch included.

But very often the singer's potential intonation can be ascertained by first discerning through audiometer tests whether the singer has acuity problems which are difficult to improve through training. Frequently these tests indicate that each ear of a singer will vary in acuity. These tests can be of considerable help to the choral director and singer in attempting to learn the extent of his pitch discrimination problems.

Sometimes a punctured ear-drum will cause an impossible situation. There is also the singer whose slovenly auditory habits acquired through poor tonal attacks will affect the production of pitch. Incorrect methods of tone production will also cause the singer to sing out of tune. His breathing may be incorrect; his tonal concept may be false, and he may conceive singing as a shouting enterprise. The ensemble's balance of parts may be such as to make a singer's hearing of the various voice parts entirely impossible. Tonality (key consciousness) will be lost. Vowel formations within words could be so distorted as to ruin tonal quality because the overtones have been vitiated. There may also be too great a number of singers on a given part, thus making the tonal and dynamic balance of the various parts well nigh impossible. Even nervous excitation will cause a singer to sing off pitch.

5. Glissando and Pitch Elision in Singing. Much pitch inaccuracy, especially in choral singing, is occasioned by "scooping" from one pitch to the next. There are many in-

dividuals who "sing with their mouth, but not with their
heads." Very often in the singing of pitches, they do not
think what they are doing and constantly confuse sequential pitch definitions. The choral director and singer must
work to eliminate this vocal habit which is responsible for
poor intonation and tone quality. Note the affect of the glissando and the elision in the following examples:

<u>Ex. I</u>

This example is a good illustration of the glissando and syllable elision frequently taking place between the syllable <u>Slid</u>
and <u>er</u>. The singer will usually bring the syllable <u>Slid</u> and
its pitch down to the syllable <u>er</u>, connecting with glissando
effect all intermediary pitches between d^2 and b^1. In actual
practice the singer does not sing a clean cut pitch at $\underline{d}^2$ for
one beat and $\underline{b}^1$ for two beats. Actually the result is that
the pronunciation becomes <u>Sli</u> and <u>Der</u> syllabically speaking.
Likewise, in the shifting of syllable metre from trochaic to
iambic, the pure intonation of $\underline{d}^2$ and $\underline{b}^1$ is lost. If this were
a choral number in which many singers were reproducing the
pitches as a simultaneous act, pitch definition would be seriously interferred with.

Ex. II

Plen   ty good   room

Example II shows the glissando pitch effect of the elision
of the word "good" to the word "room." The rapid singing
of the two words would result in false pitches between the
two words and their textual version would be goo-droom.
Not alone would the pronunciation be incorrect, but accuracy
of pitch definition for the words would have been vitiated.

Ex. III

A   -   VE   MA - RI - - -   A -

SAN - - - CTA   MA   RI - - - - A

Here are two illustrations that depict most admirably how the
glissando and pitch and word elisions could, and often do affect intonation, tone quality, and the structural metre of the
words.

Usually when "A-ve" is sung, the singer frequently car-
ries the pitch of a[1] in somewhat of a glissando manner and

superimposes it upon $b^{\flat 1}$. When this is done, it is obvious
that the definition of pitch has not been completely adhered
to for four beats on the pitch of a^1.

The portamento or the elision is sometimes prominent in
the delivery of the "ri-a" in "Maria." The incidence of the
portamento is between the syllable "ri" and "a." Its performance could be immeasurably improved if the singer
would gently settle the "ri" down on g^1, rather than overem-
phasize the portamento. It should be artistically delivered.

The "San-cta" is very much like the "Ma-ri-a" with the
exception that the interval drop is not so great. It is not
uncommon to hear a singer produce the portamento for "San-
cta" as follows:

(a)

Written

San - - - cta

(b)

Often Sung   San - - - ncta

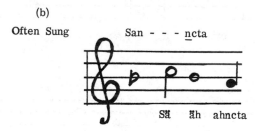

Să   ăh   ahncta

(c)

When Incorrectly Sung: Note the pitch sequences

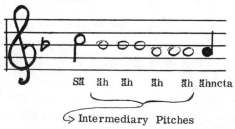

Să   ăh   ăh   ăh   ăh ăhncta

↳ Intermediary Pitches

It is apparent from the examples that the fidelity of intonation is greatly impaired when glissando and word elision are
allowed to become a part of notational reproduction. Obviously, slovenly attacks or scooping up to a given pitch by
a singer is deleterious to vocal performance. It is impossible for a choral group to sing chords of good intonation if
the pitch (tone) that is being produced is constantly being reproduced inaccurately. Good interpretation of a vocal work
is impossible if the pitch of the tones is ruined. A great
deal of a choral group's intonational problems can be re-
solved by a discriminative director. Good musicianship is
the fruition of innate musical ability and well directed choral
discipline.

   6. Mental (Nervous) Excitation. Singers suffer from
varying degrees of nervousness. Some of them never seem
to conquer excessive excitation which may seriously interfere
with the function of their singing mechanism during public
performance. The type of nervous reactions manifested by
singers varies greatly from one individual to another. Some
become so nervous as to experience severe visceral eruptions
which may even cause regurgitation. Naturally, any such
physical upheaval of the body is not going to give the singer
the vocal poise so necessary to the attainment of the art of
bel canto.

   Regardless of the degree of nervousness, whether a con-
vulsive mental and/or physical experience or only a slightly
tensed musculature, it is the job of the choral director and
vocal teacher to help these individuals to gain control of
themselves. Almost every singer is "up" a little before a
performance, but his excitation must not be so great as to
interfere with the effectiveness of his performance. As a
matter of fact, a little "edge" of exhilaration and excitation
will be beneficial to those individuals who are overly relaxed
and ineffectively demonstrative. This "upness" or "edginess"
of which we have just spoken may aid some singers to sing

with better intonation. Often the phlegmatic individual has a
tendency to sing with uncertain intonation.

   7. Constancy of Breath Flow. It is important that the
singer develop the ability to maintain an adequate breath support in order to undergird each tone with a continuing flow
of tone. In the following diagram it can be observed that the
notational and durational values of many of the notes have
been interferred with.

Pictogram of An Individual's Constancy of Breath Flow

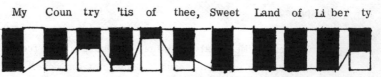

Blank areas show dynamics loss.

Pictogram of Durational Units of Breath Flow

Blank areas show durational loss.

Legend: Five Units of Volume.

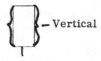
-- Vertical

Horizontal

The horizontal distance shows the durational length of breath flow.
The vertical distance shows the variations in the amount of dynamics.

   A constancy of breath (durational) flow units for tones
("America") will help to insure a legato which is both beautiful and intonationally sound. Why? Because the tones are

being supported throughout the duration of their delivery.

8. <u>Muffled Resonance Chambers and the Dropped Palate</u>.
The depressive attitude which some individuals occasionally
reflect induce a dropped palate condition that has a muffled
effect upon tone. Whenever this happens, although the veils
of the palate may be relaxed, there is a shutting off of the
main opening into the mouth cavity depriving tone of its resonance in the lower and upper pharynx region.

If the singer forces too much in the area of the throat
and sings as though he had a potato in his mouth, there may
be an element of holding the throat through rigidity of the
neck, jaw, tongue, palate, or a combination of more than
one or all of these. The tone will have an unusual amount
of excessively covered (muffled) resonance. Tones produced
under rigid muscular conditions are certain to affect the singer's ability to sing in tune. Tone produced under such conditions becomes diffused, strident, and unpleasant to the ear.
Whenever these circumstances prevail, good vowel form is
impossible. If the vowel is the purveyor of the tone, then
it is obvious that the singer's tonal timbre will suffer.

                              Notes

1. Thomas Fillebrown <u>Resonance in Singing and Speaking</u>, p.5.

2. W.J. Henderson <u>The Art of the Singer</u>, p. 90.

Chapter IV
Tone Production and Diction

It has been a common observation that diction, as a rudimentary principle of artistic singing, has been almost completely glossed over by singers in their attempt to achieve quick success. The following discussion on diction should aid both the professional as well as the beginning choral director and solo singer.

Every vocal or choral judging assignment whether it be at the local, district, regional, or state level always makes approximately the same demands upon the adjudicator's musicianly discrimination. If the performance is to be evaluated as good or inferior, diction is usually among those many considerations which are included in the making of the final selection; it also has usually been given the least attention in readying the choral ensemble or solo singer for performance.

The choral conductor and singer should be constantly concerned with the need for achieving uniformity of vowel quality if there is to be good tone production. All vowel sounds have the basic property of being musical sounds. They are the life blood of good tone quality.

The singer must always remember that in the final analysis, he can produce beautiful singing tone only through the medium of the purveyor of tone--VOWELS. Without the vowel there would be no medium for uttering vocal sounds. Thus, their pronunciation, enunciation, and articulation are the basic components of diction. An intensive study of diction and tone production will reveal there are consonants (voiced) which have tonal durational qualities. Therefore, the individuals who sing or teach singing must recognize the need for a study as to how the vowel and the consonant affect tone quality.

Basic to all good vowel singing is the need for first thinking--thinking the vowel concept and the pitch upon which it is to be sung.

84

Most beginners are slovenly tonal thinkers. There is too much
"open the mouth and no thinking" about singing. But the choral director and the singer must have a good mental image of the type of
vowel (and consonant) which they expect to be produced. Actually,
they should mentally hear ideal tone quality if they expect to produce
it. It is a fact that a person cannot sing that which he cannot hear.

Vowels of good conformation and resonation are rarely heard
in daily conversation. Most individuals produce all vowels in speech
on a horizontal plane without individual definition one from the other.
As a consequence their resonation is vitiated and the individual's
voice assumes a colorless sameness that very often approaches mo-
notony.

Vowels can be beautifully produced in English as well as in
Italian and other languages, but we do not emphasize instructional
time for this phase of speech education in our elementary and secondary schools. We have produced generations of people who are
practically ignorant of good diction. Because their ears are not at-
tuned (educated) to good vowel tone color, they are not disturbed by
their shortcomings.

Singers must be taught how to produce good vowels and they
must attune their ears to hear them. Individuals cannot sing what
they cannot hear! Good vowels supported by excellent breath support are certain to insure beautiful singing tone. It must be remembered that good pronunciation is basic to the good conformation and
quality of a vowel. Vowel formations are embodied in pronunciation.

For every vowel there is a natural tongue position. It naturally follows that for every change of a vowel there must be new adjustments (positions) in the mouth, tongue, palate, lips, and larynx.
When the singer changes abruptly from the $\bar{a}$ and $\bar{e}$ vowels (where
the larynx is in a high position) to the $\bar{o}$ and $\overline{oo}$, where the larynx
is lowered (in relation to the overall movement), the freedom of the
vocal box must be such as to facilitate ease of tonal emission. Tension of the musculature about the larynx box and tongue area must
be at a minimum.

The vowels $\bar{a}$, $\bar{e}$, $\overline{ah}$ have a tendency to draw the lips back-
ward, whereas $\overline{oo}$, $\bar{o}$, and $\bar{u}$ require forward extension of the lips.

If the singer has been properly trained and his mind is in control
of those organs responsible for good vowels and limpid pronunciation,
these lip actions are certain to assume the positions indicated.
Whenever a singer's mouth is visably distorted, and does not appear
natural and relaxed, it may be definitely assumed that internal tensions are such that good vowel formations are impossible.

Vowel Study Sequence for Training the Singer

Every choral director and singer would like to know what sequence of vowels should be used for effective study. Italian vocal
teachers of the seventeenth and eighteenth centuries almost unani-
mously preferred the vowel "ah" for initial study. About this basic
vowel they constructed their whole order of vocalizes and added the
other vowels as the singer achieved the necessary technical skill to
deliver them with good resonance and tonal timbre. The vowel "ah"
is usually more conducive to relaxing the musculature of the throat
than any of the other vowels. It must be recognized that all vowel
timbre can be altered by mental conception and attitude as well as
by partial physical adjustments such as high and low-arched palatal
singing. When this is done, the singer must fuse the thinking of o͞o
into the "ah" in order to secure a high-arched palate. There must
be a similated sensation of elevation and depth rather than breadth.
The latter always induces a spread tonal concept and flat (vowel)
mouth singing. The vowel "ah" should always produce a slight con-
caveness in the tongue (some people may prefer to call it a groove)
with the most noticeable depression felt in the mid-tongue area.
Suggestion: Very simply say ōh, and note the position of the mid
tongue. The rear of the lower jaw should feel as though it were
hanging by hinges. Complete relaxation of this area is the primary
objective.

Because most inexperienced singers lack the control to produce the "ah" sound with good tonal quality, this author prefers to
begin with "oh." It is firmly believed that it aids the beginning singer in controlling his initial tonal efforts to attain opulence and uniformity, and early attainment of good resonance. In producing "oh"
it is strongly recommended that the singer think that "u" or "oo" is

the focus position ahead of the "oh." Allow the "u" or "oo" to be
the energizing force or concept for the production of a vitalized
"oh."

Principle of Total Resonance

One major cause of poor tone production is the inability of
singers to maintain full usage of the areas available for the resonation of tone. Undoubtedly the largest open cavity is the mouth.
Rather than utilizing the entire mouth resonation for any given tone,
the inexperienced singer and many who have professional singing experience, vary the usage of the cavity nearly every time they produce tone. Rather than full chamber resonance these singers receive but partial benefits from the mouth cavity. Whereas the tonal
focus should be forward as in the sensation derived from singing a
pure o͞o or u͞, a great number of singers produce tone that is primarily resonated in the mid-mouth area or banked against the soft
palate. Too often tone is thereby engulfed or swallowed, having a
"potatoish" quality, and does not get out of the mouth. Tone must
resonate in the forward region of the mouth if it is to retain full
resonance for enhancing tonal development.

After initial work on vowel "oh," it is recommended that exercises alternating the "oh" and the "ah" be used. The purpose
is to have the singer approximate the ideal tonal concept by singing
the "oh," and then change to the "ah" repeating this in a continuous
vocalize. The singer must go from one vowel to the next without
changing the resonation of either vowel. The following exercises
are suggested:

Ex. I

Oh   ăh   ōh   ăh   OH

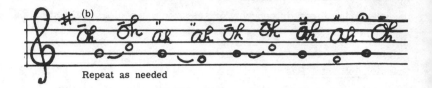

Repeat as needed

If a singer studies and applies the concepts propounded
throughout this discussion he should produce a pure vowel and rein-
force that vowel with the forward focused energization of ōō or ū.

The singer must have the ability to sustain a constant flow
of tone from one vowel or consonant articulation to the next.   He
must connect their junction (syllable or words) with as little inter-
ference as possible.   Study the following diagrams:

Ex. II

(a) 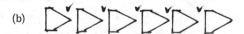 Correct

Legend: Each cube is a syllable or a word

(b)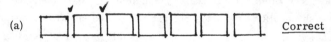

The constant tapering means loss of pitch, tone quality,
and steadiness and uniformity of tonal flow.

Diagram (a) illustrates uniformity of tonal flow and thereby assures reasonably good intonation.   Where the check
mark is placed indicates the loss of tonal flow from vowel
(also word to word) to vowel.   The check mark (✓) indicates
compactness of tonal flow.

Diagram (b) points up the loss of tonal flow when the
singer attacks tone with lack of tonal flow from vowel to
vowel.

After studying Exercises I and II, it is recommended that Exercises III and IV be used for employing the ōh and äh.

Ex. III

Oh oh, Ah ah, Oh oh, Ah   ah,

Oh   Äh

Ah   ah, Oh   oh, Ah ah, Oh oh, Ah ah, ŌH

Ex. IV

Oh   ah   Oh   ah   Oh ah, Oh ah Oh

Oh ah oh ah oh   ah oh   ah   OH

The Vowel E as in Eat or Tea

Sing <u>Exercise I</u> as frequently as desired. Say the word "Three" before singing it in order to get a feel for its position in the mouth. The vowel Ē in the word should possess a good forward (in the mask of the face) resonation. The vowel needs good energization and this is only possible if its form (concept) is purely conceived. Practice singing "Three" a number of times before going on to "Tee" and "Lee."

Ex. I

Three................................... Ē--
Tee..................................... Ē--
Lee..................................... Ē--

It is recommended that in the initial stages, the singer should sing this exercise within the most comfortable region of his voice. If <u>Exercise I</u> produces unsatisfactory results, <u>Exercise II</u> may be helpful.

Ex. II

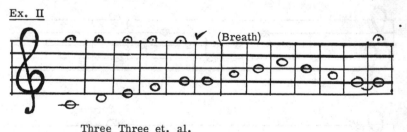

Three   Three   et. al.
Tee   Tee   et. al.
Lee   Lee   et. al.

In <u>Exercise II</u> the singer should slowly sing each syllable taking great pains to produce good vowel forms. Sing the following exercises for further training:

Ex. III

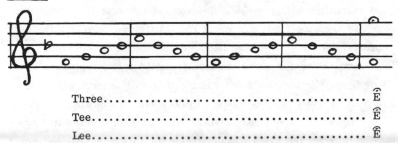

Three... Ê
Tee.. Ê
Lee.. Ê

Ex. IV

Three... Ê
Tee.. Ê
Lee.. Ê

All exercises may be sung chromatically up and down scale.

Ex. V

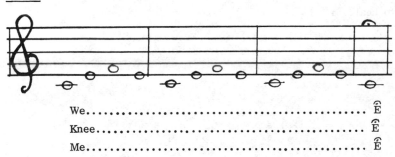

We... Ê
Knee... Ê
Me... Ê

In _Exercise V_ use words starting with the voiced consonants w, b, m, n, d, m, and n. Be sure that the vowel of the one syllable word used is long ē.

Both the choral director and singer should attempt to achieve
good resonation both for the consonant and the vowel. Always attempt to keep the focus for vowel ēē. All major vowels to be discussed are focused about the sensation derived from ōō or ū. If
the sensation for the vowel changes from the forward position of the
ōō or ū, it will lose its tonal color and it will become white, harsh,
and metalic when sung at various pitch levels of the singer's range.

Upon the expertness of vocal, diphthong, and consonant production depends the great art of singing as an intellectual and emotional medium for cultural communication. In the following pages
we have attempted to reproduce by the means of detailed Lessons
what we conceive to be some of the major vowel, diphthong, and
consonant action involved in effecting good tone quality.

The following five fundamental and subordinate vowels when
sung at any pitch should possess uniformity of timbre throughout
production. The resultant resonance and consequent tonal timbre is
only possible if tones are properly conceived forward (as in ōō or
ū) every instant they are sustained. It must be remembered that
uniformity of tonal timbre is dependent upon consistency and fidelity
of the use of those vocal techniques which are emphasized in this
series of Lessons on diction. Their continual practice will discipline the singer's ear to demand the tone quality it has been trained
to hear.

Detailed Lessons on Vowel, Consonant, and Diphthongal Action

Lesson One   Pure Vowels and Some of Their Variations.

The major or basic vowels are usually classified under the
heading of long and short vowels.   The long vowels are:

    A ā   as in Day, May

    E ē   as in Me, He

    I ī   as in Sign, Mine

    O ō‿o͞o as in Home, Boat

    U ē‿o͞o as in Cute or Lute

Each of the five major vowels is used again in words employing the short vowel form.   They are:

    A ăh as in Hat, Mat

    E ĕh as in Mend, Send

    I ĭ   as in Hit, Mit

    O ŏ   as in Pawn, Thaw

    U ŭ   as in Muss, Thus

Lesson Two   Bright Vowel E (Long Vowel).

All vowel sounds when properly sensed in the mouth seem to be naturally disposed to be delivered from either the front or back region of the mouth. The bright colored vowels are naturally sensed in the front region of the mouth.

Bright Vowels

Number	Vowel	Word
1.	ē	Meet
2.	ĭ	Mit
3.	ā	Mate
4.	ĕ	Met
5.	ă	Mat

Sensation in the frontal region of the mouth

Practice the above vowels (words) in the order given and then practice them out of their order, being especially careful to sense their regional mouth sensation.

There is another group of vowels that find their sensation region in the posterior (back) region of the mouth. They are the dark colored vowels which appear below:

Dark Vowels

Number	Vowel	Word
1.	ōō	Tool
2.	ŏŏ	Hook
3.	ō	Hold
4.	ô	Cord
5.	ä	Father

Sensation in the posterior (back) region of the mouth

Practice these dark vowels in the manner suggested for those that are positioned in the front region.

Lesson Three Exercises on Bright Vowel E (Major Vowel).

Keep in mind that bright vowels are sung with a sensation concentrated in the front area of the mouth. Sing the following exercises with medium voice. Repeat the measure once rearticulating the word or syllable.

Ex. I

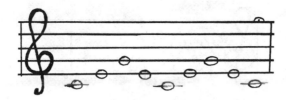

Me.......................... e
Thee .... e
Knee .... e
Tee .... e
Be .... e
Yee .... e
Lee .... e
Fee .... e

For Exercises II and III use the syllables or words to be found in Exercise I.

Ex. II

Ex. III

For <u>Exercises IV</u> and <u>V</u> use the same syllables or words used in <u>Exercise I</u>. Sing each measure twice rearticulating the vowel or word sound.

<u>Ex. IV</u>

<u>Ex. V</u>

Sing the following Bright E exercise with the consonant pre-fixes indicated below.

<u>Ex. VI</u>

Consonant Prefix	Phrase to be sung	
Voiced <u>M</u>	Me and Me are Me	
Voiced <u>B</u>	Be and Be are Be	
Explosive <u>K</u>	Knee and Knee and Knee	(The K is silent here)
Explosive <u>T</u>	Tee and Tee are Tee	
Voiced Explosive <u>L</u>	Lee and Lee are Lee	
Sibilant <u>F</u>	Fee and Fee are Fee	

Lesson Four   Bright Vowel I (Short Vowel).

Sing all the following exercises as continuous phrases with one breath.   Move all Exercises chromatically up and down the scale.

Ex. I

Me........ Mit........ Thee
We........ Bit .... Thee
Ye .... Fit .... Thee

In this exercise we are first using a word with a previously practiced vowel.   Then follow it with a word containing a new vowel to be included for study and practice.

Ex. II

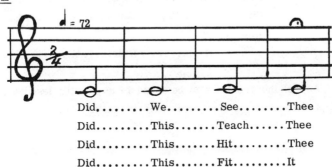

Did.........We.........See........Thee
Did.........This.......Teach......Thee
Did.........This.......Hit.........Thee
Did.........This.......Fit.........It

It is hoped that through this exercise it will be possible to keep the vowel Ĭ from spreading from its true (natural) form.

Ex. III

```
Sin........Is.........Sin
Sit........In.........Mist
Did .......It ..........Sing
King ......Is.........King
```

The exercise below incorporates the usage of all words with the vowel Y.

Ex. IV

```
Sin......is...........Sin......is........Sin
Sit......in...........Sin......in.......Mist
King....is...........King.....is.......King
Did.....it...........Did......it.......Sing
```

Any of the vocalizes to be found in any of the lessons may be adapted to augment these exercises in Lesson Four.

<u>Lesson Five</u>   Bright Vowel A (Long Vowel Containing Diphthongal
            Sound ĕ).

This fundamental or basic vowel is actually a compound vowel
possessing two sounds when it is properly delivered.   Actually, the
vowel ā sounds ā̯ ĭ (ĕ) as in day (ĕ̯ ĭ).   Keep in mind that the major
vowels (ā, ī, ō, ū) excepting ē, are compound or diphthongs written
as one vowel (letter) having two phonetic sounds.   The diphthong is
always written with two letters.

<u>Ex. I</u>

Day,   Day,   Day,   Day,   Day
May,   May,   May,   May,   May
Say,   Say,   Say,   Say,   Say
Way,   Way,   Way,   Way,   Way
Bay,   Bay,   Bay,   Bay,   Bay

Because these exercises include words containing the basic
vowel ā (ĕ), the singer should be careful to prolong it, giving but a
momentary prolongation to the subordinate diphthongal sound of (ē).

<u>Ex. II</u>

Lay.........................ā (ĕ̯ ĭ)
May ....ā
Way ....ā
Bay.........................ā
Day.........................ā

Any of these Exercises may be repeated for the development
of tonal control.

Ex. III

Lay ā   May ā   Way ā   Bay   ā   Dāy

When singing the vowel (eliding it from one pitch to another) on all pitches and especially on the second and fourth counts of each measure, the singer should be extremely careful to retain the purity of the fundamental vowel imbedded in each word, (ĕ ĭ) which is ā.

The singer must always keep in mind that the pronunciation of the words must be distinct and they must be intelligible to the hearer.

Always sing Exercises with one breath.

Ex. IV

Lay.............................ā (ĕ ĭ)
May ....ā
Way ....ā
Bay............................ā
Day............................ā
Nay............................ā

If the vowel ā is held too long, the subordinate vowel sounds increasingly more like (ē).

Ex. V

Lay.....................................ā (ĕ ĭ)

May ....ā

Way ....ā

Bay.....................................ā

Day.....................................ā

Nay.....................................ā

<u>Lesson Six</u>   Bright Vowel ĕ (Short Vowel).

    This bright vowel is like ĕ in fed or ĕ in end. It is very easy to substitute the short ŭ as in hĕlped (hulp) for the short ĕ. There are a great number of words where the perversion of the short ĕ results in the short ŭ.

self	sŭlf	for sĕlf
bell	bŭll	for bĕll
dell	dŭll	for dĕll
let	lŭt	for lĕt
fell	fŭll	for fĕll
felt (better)	fŭlt	for fĕlt

    Sing these Exercises with great care, listening carefully for any tendency to substitute the incorrect short vowel (ŭ) for ĕ.

<u>Ex. I</u>   Move Exercise up and down scale.

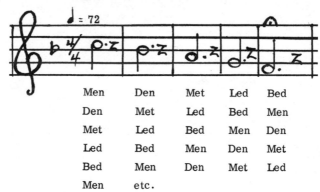

Men	Den	Met	Led	Bed
Den	Met	Led	Bed	Men
Met	Led	Bed	Men	Den
Led	Bed	Men	Den	Met
Bed	Men	Den	Met	Led
Men	etc.			

Ex. II   Be certain that the flow of tone is steady.

Pĕn...................................ĕn
Dĕn...................................ĕn
Bĕd...................................ĕd
Lĕd...................................ĕd

Ex. III

Mĕ(t).............ĕt   Nĕ(t)...............ĕt
Nĕ(t).............ĕt   Nĕ(d)...............ĕd

Ex. IV

Lĕ(d)....................................ĕd
Mĕ(t)....................................ĕt
Nĕ(t) ....ĕt
Bĕ(d)....................................ĕd

Ex. V

Mět..ět

Nět..ět

Lěd..ěd

Běd..ěd

Lesson Seven   Bright Vowel A (Short Vowel).

Ex. I

```
Măt.....................................ăt
Năn.....................................ăn
Măn ....................................ăn
Dăm.....................................ăm
```

Ex. II

```
Măt.....................................ăt
Năn.....................................ăn
Făn.....................................ăn
Văn.....................................ăn
```

In all of these exercises, regardless of the lesson number, it is urged that the singer emphasize strongly the voiced or non-voiced consonant at the beginning of each word or syllable. A word or syllable is usually begun with a voiced consonant because of its vocal possibilities.

Ex. III

Năn...............ăn   Măn.................ăn
Măd ....ăd   Măn.................ăn
Dăn...............ăn   Măn.................ăn
Văn...............ăn   Măn.................ăn

Ex. IV

Măn.................ăn   Măn.................ăn
Dăd ....ăd   Dăd ....ăd
Văn.................ăn   Văn ....ăn
Năn.................ăn   Năn ....ăn

Ex. V

Man...............ân   Man.................ân
Dad................ad   Dad ....ad
Van ....an   Van.................an
Nan ....an   Nan.................an

<u>Lesson Eight</u>   Dark Vowel OO (Long Vowel).

<u>Ex. I</u>

Wōo.....................................ōo
Sōon ....ōoN*
Bōom ....ōoM*
Mōon ....ōoN*
Nōon ....ōoN*

*Emphasize wherever possible the voiced consonant. In these
exercises the syllable or word to be sung is indicated, but the singer is expected to sustain only the pure vowel (in this case oo) and
finish the exercise with a strongly resonated consonant.

<u>Ex. II</u>

Lōo.................................ōo
Dōo.................................ōo
Bōo.................................ōo
Mōo ....ōo
Wōo ....ōo

Ex. III

Loo...................................oo

Doo...................................oo

Boo...................................oo

Moo...................................oo

Woo...................................oo

Ex. IV

Boom...............................ooM

Noon ....ooN

Loon ....ooN

Doom...............................ooM

Zoom...............................ooM

Lesson Nine   Dark Vowel OO (Short Vowel).

Ex. I

Bŭll........ŏoL	Bŭll............ŏoL
Fŭll........ŏoL	Fŭll............ŏoL
Wŏod.......ŏoD	Wŏod...........ŏoD
Gŏod.......ŏoD	Gŏod...........ŏoD

Ex. II

| Bŭll.........................ŏoL |
| Fŭll.........................ŏoL |
| Wŏod........................ŏoD |
| Gŏod........................ŏoD |
| Wŏuld.......................ŏoD |

Ex. III

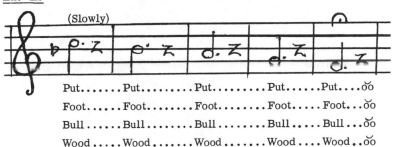

| Put.......Put.........Put.........Put......Put....ŏo |
| Foot......Foot........Foot........Foot.....Foot...ŏo |
| Bull......Bull........Bull........Bull.....Bull...ŏo |
| Wood.....Wood.......Wood.......Wood....Wood..ŏo |

After the singer has practiced as suggested, it is recommended that each step of the exercise employ a different word from

the one which is used at the beginning.

Ex. IV

Put...ŏŏ
Foot..ŏŏ
Bull..ŏŏ
Wood..ŏŏ
Could ....ŏŏ

<u>Lesson Ten</u> Dark Vowel Ō (Long Vowel).

Vowel Ō is another compound vowel possessing one vowel but two sounds, resulting in Ō‿ŎŎ if the singer moves the mouth to a closing position while sustaining the pure Ō. The open mouth form Ō must not change position during its production.

Ex. I

Do..Ō
Mo ....Ō
Go..Ō
No..Ō

Ex. II

Dome.................................ōM
Moan.................................ōN
Loam.................................ōM
Roam.................................ōM

The need for limited or extended breath in all exercises is dependent upon the tempo at which they are sung.

Ex. III

Mold..........ōLD	Mold...............ōLD
Bold...........ōLD	Bold...............ōLD
Wold..........ōLD	Wold...............ōLD
Roam.......... ōM	Roam.............. ōM
Moan .... ōN	Moan.............. ōN

Ex. IV

Move chromatically up and down the scale to suit individual needs.

Mold...ōLD
Bold..ōLD
Wold...ōLD
Roam... ōM
Moan .... ōN

Lesson Eleven Dark Vowel Ô (Short Vowel).

Ex. I

Take breath as needed.

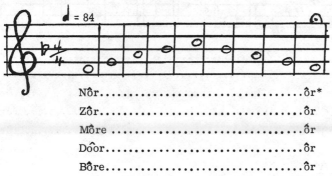

Nôr.................................ôr*
Zôr.................................ôr
Môre ....ôr
Dôor.................................ôr
Bôre.................................ôr

*Do not burr or roll the r.

Ex. II

Zôr...... For...... More...... Door...... Bore
Fôr...... More ....Door ...... Bore...... Zor
Môre ....Door..... Bore ...... Zor....... For
Dôor..... Bore..... Zor .... For....... More
Bôre..... Zor...... For....... More ..... Door

Ex. III

Zôr.....................................ôr
Fôr.....................................ôr
Môre ....ôr
Dóor....................................ôr
Bôre....................................ôr

Ex. IV

Zôr	Zor	Zor	Zor	ôr
Fôr	For	For	For	ôr
Môre	More	More	More	ôr
Dóor	Door	Door	Door	ôr
Bôre	Bore	Bore	Bore	ôr

Lesson Twelve   Dark Vowel Ä (Long Vowel).

     This long vowel (ä) is another compound vowel. It is diph-
thongal in that it possesses two vowel sounds for one letter (äh ĭ).
The singer should sustain the äh part of the vowel, and deemphasize
the ĭ. The metre of the vowel delivery should be trochaic ___ ˘
rather than iambic ˘ ___ .

Ex. I

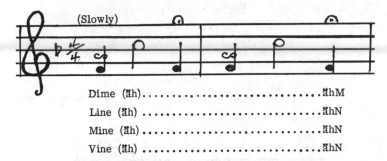

Dime (äh)..............................ähM
Line (äh) ....ähN
Mine (äh)..............................ähN
Vine (äh) ....ähN

Ex. II

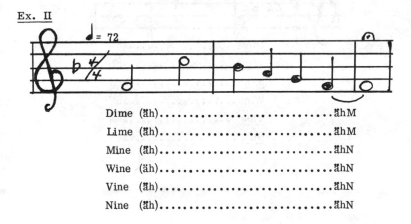

Dime (äh)..............................ähM
Lime (äh)..............................ähM
Mine (äh)..............................ähN
Wine (äh)..............................ähN
Vine (äh)..............................ähN
Nine (äh)..............................ähN

     Be certain to emphasize the vowel (äh) when connecting the
interval of a fifth (f^1-c^2).

Ex. III

```
Dime................ăhM
Lime................ăhM
Mine................ăhN
Wire ...............ăhN
Vine ...............ăhN
Nine ...............ăhN
```

Ex. IV

The singer must emphasize the voiced consonants which are underscored.

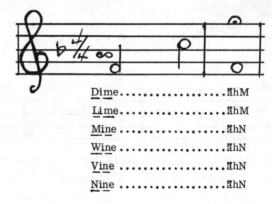

```
Dime................ăhM
Lime................ăhM
Mine................ăhN
Wine................ăhN
Vine ...............ăhN
Nine ...............ăhN
```

Lesson Thirteen Diphthongs.

In our discussion of the five major vowels (Lessons 1-12),
ā, ē, ī, ō, ū, it was stated that each of them (except ē), when produced has a diphthongal sound. The reader is not to confuse the
vowels and the subordinate diphthongal sounds with the real diphthong
which has two vowels (not sounds). Every compound vowel has a
long (sustained) and a short sound.

In addition to the four major vowels that have diphthongal
sounds there are two diphthongs ou and oi that frequently appear in
words. Here we have a two letter diphthong which distinguishes itself by its spelling. Diphthongs, whether by one letter sounds or
two letter spellings, may be enumerated according to the following
chart from Clara Kathleen Rogers' English Diction (p. 62):

Diphthong Chart (One letter sound and two letter words)
1. (I)   a   (ăh͜'ē) aisle
2.   oi)*   (ău'ē) oil
3.   ou)   (ă' o͞o) out
4. (A)   ā   (ā' ē) play, aid
5. (O)   ō   (ō' o͞o) woe
6. (U)   u   (ē o͞o) ewe

*Not imbedded among compound sounds

Illus. I Compound Vowel Sounds in Words of One Letter Diphthongs.

Tight	ă͜ e͞et
Nine	ă͜ e͞en
Isle	ă͜ e͞el
Owe	ŏ o͞o
Bold	ō ŏ͞o
Soul	ō ŏ͞o
Loaf	ō o͝o

Illus. II   Compound Vowels in Words of Two Letter Diphthongs.

Pie	ă̱ē	(ĭ)*	*Another vowel phonetic
Pay	ā̱ē	(ĭ)	sound possibility.
Thou	ă̱o͞o		
Create	ē ā	(ĭ)	
Coil	au ĭl		
Join	aw ĭ		
Oil	aw (au) ē͞el		

As the singer must sustain the long or major vowels, he should study the fundamental and subordinate sounds in all words. Too many singers ruin their tonal vowel delivery because they sustain subordinate vowels at the expense of the fundamental vowel. Any student of diction will readily discern that the great number of words containing diphthongal sounds and diphthongal letters will need more than passing attention by the singer.

Voices of potential beauty very often never attain their full tonal development because of poor vowel and diphthong understanding. Actually, many singing teachers themselves have not been trained to fully understand the close relationship existing between good vowel and diphthong production and singing tone.

The poor delivery of English words may be largely attributed to the lack of awareness, or understanding, of the impact of the diphthong upon good diction and tonal timbre. Much speech instruction totally ignores the importance of this significant aspect of diction.

Lesson Fourteen Pure Vowels and their Modification.

The modification of the major vowels is necessary in the various registers of a singer's voice. The variation or amount of modification varies slightly from one singer to another due to the range and timbre of his voice. It is the discriminative ear of the choral director and teacher of singing which will determine the nature and degree of the modification. Every singer is not able to hear his own voice with the same critical discrimination as his teacher.

Some of the more important modifications are:

1. The vowel o͞o (bo͞ot) as pronounced in whoop or whom, in the mid-lower mouth-chest register is often modified to o͝o as in lo͝ok, in the lower chest register.

2. The vowel ē as pronounced in sēēp, in the middle-lower, middle, and middle-upper register is frequently modified slightly to ĕh as in dreaming. The vowel ĕh (ĕ ̱ā) for dreaming would imply a slightly opened mouth instead of the very tight form for ē in sēēp. Thus, in the singing of high pitches, some voices would probably approach dreaming as drêam (ûh)ing. All voices must be closely studied in order to suggest at what pitch the singer must make slight vowel modifications. This modification varies slightly with voices of all classifications at all pitch levels.

The modification of ē very frequently can assume the sound of the German ü in the low register of deep male voices and less frequently in the female mezzo soprano and contralto. The ü may possess the sensation of being more elliptical in the low register.

The singer must be careful to have the larynx (throat) completely free, with no stiffness while singing. The singer should practice singing simple vocalizes alternating the vowel ē with äh and o͞o. These vowels will give the singer an opportunity to experience the variations in the positions of larynx from

high to low. The singer should be watchful of the
tone assuming a nasal quality. In addition, he should
practice these vowels as found in single syllable words.
The singer should always practice the suggested exercises very slowly when he is attempting to achieve
idealistic tone quality. He should keep in mind that
the larynx (voice box), tongue, lower jaw, and musculature of the neck should be relaxed during all singing.

3. Vowel ā sometimes presents problems because of the
singer's tendency to flatten its form too much while
employing it in the singing of ascending pitches. By
employing an ā which is halfway between ĕh and ûh,
(ĕhûh) the singer can produce more effective resonant
tones. He should assume an attitude of (elevated) in-
spiration--even exhilaration may more closely describe
the state of mental attitude which is essential to the
singing of this vowel in a desirable manner. This
elevated attitude will have a tendency to elevate the
palate.

4. Vowel ī, like ă has the same tendency to flatten in
the upper range of the singer's voice. This vowel
(ī), pronounced ăh (rounded form), should assume a
halfway sound between ăh and ăwh (ăh-awn). The forward sensation (placement sensation) described previously must always be preeminent in the production
of all vowels discussed under 1, 2, 3, and 4.

<u>Lesson Fifteen</u>   Need for Vowel Sustainment.

Many words require duality of vowel delivery; this is due primarily to their peculiar structure. These conditions are even found in one syllable words; the first vowel being long and the second short. The following illustrations indicate their existence.

<u>Illus. I</u>

Mine	Mīh	ēN
Toy	Toi	ē
Mound	Mā	o͞o
Say	Sā	ē
Now	Nau	o͞o

There is another group of words where the short vowel is heard and delivered rapidly, whereas the second vowel receives the greater sustainment.

<u>Illus. II</u>

Mew	mē	o͞o.........
Pew	pē	o͞o.........
Queen	Qo͞o	ēN ....
Quite	Qo͞o	āh.........ēt

All vowels are sensed and thereby functionally formed in the throat. It will be helpful to the singer if he will <u>sense</u>* the following vowels in an aspirated manner in the sequence on p. 122.

Äh,   Ā,   Ē,   Ī,   Ō,   OŌ
1   2   3   4   5   6

Say each vowel over many times before going on to the next vowel.
After the vowels have been articulated as suggested, then practice
them in the combinations as suggested by the numbers:

1. 1 -- 6   5. 5 -- 3
2. 2 -- 6   6. 6 -- 2
3. 3 -- 5   7. 6 -- 1
4. 4 -- 4

*Keep the mouth open, articulating the vowels but not
vocally. They are only heard in an aspirated or
breathy manner.

Slow thoughtful and patient practice of these one syllable word
exercises (containing diphthongs) will prove helpful to the singer.
Vowels that give the impression that they are formed or made in the
mouth are certain to interfere with their true or distinct nature. It
is more desirable that their pure form be properly conceived or
sensed in the mind. The singer must remember that vowels as purveyors of tone are to receive their functional form in the mouth,
but it is stressed that their purity of mouth form depends entirely
upon the fidelity of the nature of the singer's mental concept of the
vowels. Naturally, great care should be exercised in singing vowels.
The continual moving of the lower jaw while sustaining a vowel must
be eliminated.

Lesson Sixteen   Vowels--Their Relation to Tongue and Larynx
                 Position.

Registers and their respective pitch ranges affect larynx and
palate levels, consequently, their positions are in large part responsible for vowel (tonal) sounds.   Try these words and observe the
effect they have on larynx positions.   Say the words very slowly using them in the order suggested.

            Ex. I   Deep Larynx Position (Sensation) o͞o
                        Do͞om
                        Mo͞on
                        Lo͞on
                        Ro͞om

        Ex. II   High Larynx Position (Sensation) e͞e
                        Se͞em
                        De͞em
                        Re͞eme
                        Te͞en
                        Pre͞en
                        Dre͞en
Alternate the saying of the words in Ex. II with those in Ex. I.

            Ex. III   Mid Lower Larynx Position (Sensation) Ō h
                        Ōmen
                        Ōwn
                        Ōpen
                        Ōld

            Ex. IV   Middle Larynx Position (Sensation) Ā
                        Āim
                        Āte
                        Āge
                        Āgent

<u>Ex. V</u>   <u>High Larynx Position</u> (Sensation) Ē
Ēven
Ēat
Ēqual
Ēther

The singer should understand that between these major vowel positions there are intermediary positions such as induced by ĕh and ăh. The former (ĕh) would produce a mid-high position and ăh a high mid-position sensed directly above ā.

The various tongue (major and modified forms) positions for all vowels are directly related to these larynx actions. The singer capable of producing beautiful tones must of necessity sense each vowel in order that the tongue position and larynx action do not interfere with the natural action of these organs involved in singing. Their normal action (function) must be closely studied and aided by thoughtful study if there is to be good tone. The tongue and the larynx are attached to each other, thereby indicating the close relationship of these organs in the process of singing.

It is imperative that the singer practice the sensing of these tongue positions (see Exercises I-V) in order that they will be automatically assumed whenever their use is employed in singing. The positions are important if proper vocal techniques are to be facilitated. The correct tongue and larynx positions are automatic, but the singer must recognize and understand their true functions. The teacher of singing must attempt to aid the singer to achieve normal vocal actions. Such actions will induce correct tongue and larynx positions.

Lesson Seventeen Consonants.

There are twenty-one consonants in the English alphabet which
are too often overlooked by the choral director and the singer.
Voice study frequently ignores even their casual consideration. This
slighting of the consonant is most understandable because it is the
vowel that is basically so vocal.

It is the consonant which governs the articulateness of speech.
However, because it may temporarily obstruct or interrupt the free
flow of singing tone, its influence upon the flow of vocal tone must
be studied. This situation necessitates that the singer make a determined study of how the various consonants influence the media of
vocal communication--speaking and singing. Once the singer under-
stands the function of the consonants in relation to effective vocal
sound there should be a marked improvement in his singing. It
should be reassuring to the singer to know that good diction and superior tone quality can be fused into one singular unified tonal result. Generally speaking, consonants determine word meaning, yet
as a rule have insignificant duration. Whereas the vowels monopo-
lize sound duration in words, the consonants contribute form or out-
line to context.

Facts About Consonants. The major consonant groupings are
voiced and voiceless. Included among the voiced group are: B, R,
M, N, L, G, J, D, V, W, Y, Z, ẞ , ʒ , ʤ , ŋ ; voiceless consonants are expressed by the usage of F, K, P, T, H, S, θ, ʃ .
Voiced consonants have vocal or tonal resonation possibilities.
Place the thumb on one side of the larynx box and index finger on
the opposite side. Pronounce man then tip and notice the amount
of resonation in the larynx box as to its total absence in the latter
word.

Voiceless consonants lack the resonation and tonal purveying
ability possessed by the voiced consonants. The position of the consonants in a word have considerable affect on the degree of their
resonation. A voiced or voiceless consonant at the beginning of a
word has the opposite stress when it is used as a word ending.
These consonants can have anterior, mid-mouth, and posterior pro-

duction sensations that affect the consonant stress, such as:

Consonant	Anterior	Mid-Mouth	Posterior
M	Mean	Tame	Dim

These variations may be found prevalent in all of the consonants we have classified.

The following consonant category groups are quite commonly used to indicate the manner in which physical organs articulate them.

Consonant Category	Consonant
Aspirate	H
Explosive	K, T, P, G, D, B, J, W, Y
Fricative	F, V, Z, Th, H, S (Open Consonants)
Lingual	L, R, Th
Nasal	M, N
Sibilant	S, Sh, Zh, Ch, Th

Explanation:

Aspirate has a breathy quality and a non-vocalized character in hearing its production.

Explosive (Plosive) involves explosion of breath that has been withheld of expulsion.

Fricative has a frictional production because the breath is forced between the teeth in delivery.

Lingual employs considerable tongue action in its delivery.

Sibilant allows a gentle flow of breath to pass through the mid-mouth area.

Extremely helpful is the appended consonant classification according to the organs employed in their delivery. The classifications are determined by the point of articulatory function and the resultant area of obstruction.

Consonant Classification by Organic Function[1]

Classification					Organs Used

1. Bi-Labial:

p	All as initial consonants			put	Two lips are used
b	"	"	"	"	bit
w	"	"	"	"	win
m	"	"	"	"	mit

2. Labio-Dental:

f	All as initial consonants			fun	Basically lower lip and teeth
v	"	"	"	"	vine	are employed

3. Lingua-Dental:

ɵ	All as initial consonants			thine	
ð	"	"	"	"	the	Tip of tongue and the teeth

4. Lingua-Alveolar:

l	As initial consonant			let	Produced by tip of tongue and dental or alveolar ridge
t	"	"	"	tip	Spread tongue and the dental ridge
d	"	"	"	dip	
n	"	"	"	not	
s	"	"	"	sit	Spread tongue and the dental ridge
z	As final consonant			his	Tip of tongue and supported by teeth
ʃ	As initial consonants in			shun	Produced by sideways action of tongue and dental ridge
ʒ	As final consonant in			pleasure	Produced by tip of tongue and teeth
ʧ	As initial consonant in			rib	Produced by sides of tongue and the dental ridge

5. Lingua-Palatal:

j	As initial consonant in			jest	Tongue sideways action and hard palate

[1]James Milton O'Neil and Andrew Thomas Weaver, The Elements of Speech. (Chicago, Illinois: Longmans, Green and Co., 1926). Much assistance derived from Chapter VII, pages 131-132.

Classification	Organs Used
6. Lingua-Velar:	
k As initial consonant in kick	Posterior action of tongue and soft palate
g " " " " go	
ŋ As final consonant in ring	
7. Glottal:	
h As initial consonant in hot	Breathy glottal action

The following classification of consonants have been categorized as having silent, less-voiced, or voiced tonal resonation potentials. There is a significant difference in a consonant's resonation when it is used at the beginning or at the end of a word.

Classification of Consonant Sounds
Word Beginnings

Consonant Beginning	Beginning of Word	Grouping	Classification
F	Fun	Voiceless	Fricative
K	Kick	Voiceless	Explosive
K	Knee	Silent K	--
P	Part, Pup	Voiceless	Explosive
T	Top, Tin	Voiceless	Explosive
H	Hate, Hat	Voiceless	Aspirate
B	Box, Boy	Less-Voiced	Explosive
M	More, Mile	Less-Voiced	Nasal
N	Now, New	Less-Voiced	Nasal
L	Lose, Leak	Less-Voiced	Lingual
R	Red, Run, Round	Voiced	Lingual
G	Go	Voiced	Explosive
J or G	Gem, Jump	Less-Voiced	Explosive
D	Dog	Less-Voiced	Explosive
V	Vine, Voice	Voiced	Fricative
W	Win, Window	Less-Voiced	Explosive
Y	Yew, Yet	Less-Voiced	Explosive
Z	Zoo, Zero	Less-Voiced	Fricative

Legend: Silent Consonant: So designated a consonant receives no articulation or resonation.

Less-Voiced: So designated a consonant that is termed less-voiced has considerably weaker resonation.

Voiced: So designated a consonant that is designated voiced has considerable tonal resonation.

Classification of Consonant Sounds
Word Endings

Consonant	Ending of Word	Grouping	Classification
F	Leaf	Voiced	Fricative
K	Black	Voiceless	Explosive
K	(See above)	--	--
P	Leap, Reap	Voiceless	Explosive
T	Pit, Sit	Voiceless	Explosive
H	Cash, Lash	Voiceless	Aspirate
B	Bub, Bob	Voiced	Explosive
M	Ram, Dam	Voiced	Nasal
N	Fun, Men	Voiced	Nasal
L	Will, Fall	Voiced	Lingual
R	Far, Star, Mar	Voiced	Lingual
G	Rug	Voiced	Explosive
J or G	Fudge	Voiced	Explosive
D	Raid, Fade	Voiced	Explosive
V	Love, Rove, Dove	Voiced	Fricative
W	Low, Grow	Voiced	Explosive
Y	Hay, May (when it follows vowel)	Non-voiced	Explosive
Z	Size, Maze	Voiced	Fricative

Legend: Silent Consonant: So designated a consonant receives no articulation or resonation.

Less-Voiced: So designated a consonant that is termed less-voiced has considerably weaker resonation.

Voiced: So designated a consonant that is designated voiced has considerable tonal resonation.

Lesson Eighteen Consonants Requiring Pronounced Lip Action.

There are many consonants that require active or pronounced lip action. They are: b, f, m, p, v, w, wh. Connected with these lip consonants are many problems.

1. When B is joined with other consonants, lip preciseness is imperative.

Br	Broke	Bl	Bloom
Bl	Blown	Br	Brown

2. F requires a preciseness of delivery. Too much breath passing between the lips causes a poor quality of consonant.

Fl	Flame	Fl	Flown
Fr	Fringe	Fr	Frown

3. M is unique in that it requires tone for its emission. It is a voiced consonant, thus giving it vocal sound. The lips must come together expertly, lightly, and with dispatch.

   Say the following: My, Man, Moon, Moan, May

4. P requires diaphragmatic and abdominal pressure just prior to the delivery of the consonant, followed by a vowel sound or consonant.

Pl	Plane	Pr	Proud
Pa	Paint	Pe	Peat

5. V is a voiced consonant with a rumbling noise which is or should be supported by the diaphragm. It is possible that the support for the V is above that needed for the P. Letter V is always followed by a vowel in the English language.

Vine	Vote
Vow	View

6. <u>W</u> is a voiced consonant which gets its great delivery momentum from strong pursed lip movements. Simultaneously the cheeks become hollowed. There is a rumbling sound in its precise delivery which must be amply supported by the diaphragm.

We	Wand	Win
Wine	Wink	Wang

7. <u>Wh</u> (Digraph--two consonants representing one sound) is very much like <u>W</u>. Its delivery always appears to be very breathy. A precise delivery requires lip action and good abdominal and diaphragmatic support.

Whine	Whip
White	What

Lesson Nineteen Consonants Requiring Pronounced Tongue Action.

1. D requires that the tongue be pressed anteriorly against the roof of the mouth until its expulsion. There is no need for special diaphragmatic support. After the delivery of D, there is always the whispered or partially breathy tonal sound of "uh," as in the syllable "duh." Experiment saying the following words in which D may be followed by vowels, consonants, or come at the end of a word.

Don't	Done	Did	Dime
Drop	Drink	Drone	Dream
Bold	Mold	Bad	Cleaved

It is quite common for many singers to sound D instead of T when it occurs at the end of certain syllables or words.

> Sidding for Sitting
> Liddle for Little
> Seddle for Settle

It is recommended that a dramatic hesitancy be employed before saying the T or D. Thinking about what is to be sung will aid in the singing of a word. Again study the following:

> Dat for Dad
> Pad for Pat
> Shout he for Should he
> Cout she for Could she
> Mut for Mud

2. J requires diaphragmatic support. There should be a slight anterior pressure of the tongue against the teeth. The tongue braces itself before there is emission of the consonant. There is a lower larynx rumble preceded by a somewhat breathy hissing sound.

Joy	Jump	Jive
June	Joke	

3. <u>L</u> again requires the diaphragm to harden. The tongue is raised and pressed against the hard palate in front of the upper teeth. The rumbling sound is again in evidence. The tongue should be kept forward; if tongue is in posterior region the consonant may sound like a rolled or guttural <u>r</u>.

Lay	Long	Lewd
Low	Let	Lie

4. <u>N</u>. This voiced consonant needs diaphragmatic support for good resonation. In its delivery the tongue must be pressed against the roof of the mouth just back of the front teeth and braced against the hard palate. In order to produce the <u>N</u> properly, there is a glottal attack or "check" in the throat before it is delivered. This consonant has a nasal quality. Practice saying the following words where <u>N</u> is used as a beginning and as a final consonant.

Noun	Not	Born	Won	Corn
Nose	Nome	Town	Loan	
Name	Nit	Worn	Lean	

5. <u>Q</u> (ē-o͝o). This consonant cannot be articulated without the vowel (u) (ē-o͝o) following it. Its delivery always necessitates a puckering of facial features--the lips and cheeks reveal this condition. The mouth opening is characteristic of that described for the vowel ē, but more elliptical as required for o͞o. The tongue is spread, encompassing the entire floor area of the mouth. It is slightly braced for the expulsion of this consonant.

Quick	Quote
Quiet	Quire
Queen	

Diction

35

. <u>R.</u> The delivery of this consonant by the tongue varies differently depending upon its position in a word:

(a) When <u>r</u> is the first letter of the word. This positioned <u>r</u> may be termed the soft <u>r</u>. The lower jaw should relax on its downward movement for uttering the consonant. There is a drawing back of the tongue and need for slight diaphragmatic support to aid its propulsion. Note that a vowel sound precedes the articulation of this consonant, emphasizing the need for opening the mouth (äh-r). This pre-vowel is not apparent when <u>r</u> is followed by a vowel.

Run	Rind
Ruin	Ring
Rat	Race

(b) When <u>r</u> is followed by a consonant. When singing an English text, it is generally conceded that when the <u>r</u> is followed by a consonant, it is not rolled, but rather it becomes a soft <u>r</u> preceded by äh as in these words:

Farm Alarm Darn

The vowel äh is changed in some words to other modified vowels which suffix the <u>r</u> as in:

Dorn	Burn
Morn	Firm

It must be noted that the <u>r</u> is still soft, unrolled, and not overly guttural.

(c) When <u>r</u> is at the end of a word. For the singer who must project words with distinctness, the final <u>r</u> which always follows vowels, presents a new problem for ending such words. The final <u>r</u> as in words like Car, Bar, etc., is concluded with a slight ûh. The ûh may vary to an äh but the sound following the final <u>r</u> is somewhere between ûh and äh. Final clarity of a word may necessitate the need for the suffixed vowel sound.

Bar	Tar
Car	Far
Mar	

(d) When r precedes a vowel in words of two or more syllables. When this occurs it will be noted that the r starts the second syllable as in:

Mary	Very
Dora	Berry

Practice these and other words to observe the sound of the r being the same as when it starts a word. See discussion under (a).

(e) When a double rr appears in a word, the first r ends a syllable and the second r starts another syllable. The rule to apply to the first r is the same as when it ends a one syllable word; the rule for the second r would be the same as when it starts a word.

Carry	Tarry
Marry	Arrow
Ferry	

7. S. This consonant requires a flattened tongue, with lips drawn to the side of the mouth. The diaphragm must aid in the propulsion of the air (breath) out of the mouth. The air appears to strike the upper rather than the lower teeth. The tongue must be firm in its mouth position while the consonant is being propelled out of the mouth. Be sure that the stroke of the s is precise and not drawn out or it will produce an annoying hissing sound.

Sun	Shine	Soon	Saw
Son	Sit	Soul	
Shone	Short	Same	

8. <u>T</u>. This consonant requires that a vowel be suffixed to it if it is to be delivered. The tongue must be projected against the entire anterior and mid-hard palate area before its propulsion. Good diaphragmatic support is needed for a crisp delivery.

Tip	Tune
Top	Time
Toe	Tank

9. <u>Y</u>. This consonant may be more accurately described as possessed of a combination of <u>we</u> (w äh ē). It needs deep diaphragmatic support for good projection. The tongue is spread out in the flat of the mouth and the lips are partially drawn backwards. Try these examples:

Yam	Young
Yak	You
Yet	Yule

10. <u>Z</u>. When saying <u>z</u>, the lips are drawn backwards and the teeth are barely separated. The tongue touches the lower more than the upper teeth during its delivery. It must be delivered with crispness or there may develop the hissing sound so often found in the projection of the consonant <u>S</u>.

Zinc	Zebra	Lose
Puzzle	Zephyr	
Zif	Buzz	

*11. <u>NG</u>. Frequently the <u>NG</u> is not clearly defined. The following are typical errors in the pronunciation of words containing this digraph:

Sittin'	for Sitting	
Rowin'	for Rowing	*<u>NG</u> does not occur at
Bowin'	for Bowing	the beginning of a word
Mowin'	for Mowing	
Singin'	for Singing	

The way to correct most of this trouble is to have the
tongue propelled against the posterior hard palate and soft
palate areas. Nasality is always characteristic of a well
produced NG.

12. CH.   The tongue is pressed against the hard palate for
this digraph.   The tongue actually encompasses the whole
of the palatal area.   It is braced against the palate just
before the digraph delivery.   There must be reasonably
good diaphragmatic support for a good ejaculation of the
CH.   When CH appears at the beginning of a word, there
is a breathy-whispered sound that accompanies its delivery.
Practice the following by using the simple exercise which
has been suggested for use.

Churn....................
Charm...................
Cheek...................
Chinck...................

When the Digraph CH concludes the word it has a breathy
or whispering sound.   The singer should study and practice the following:

    Patch   Match   Such
    Latch   Much   Search

13. SH.   In order to produce this digraph the tongue is pressed
lightly against the anterior area of the hard palate.   A
seemingly breathy escape of air appears to constitute its
total pronounced structure.   There is a definite whispering
quality apparent in delivery.   Employing the vocal exercise
suggested immediately above using the following words

should prove worthwhile.

Share	Shame	Mash	Dash
Shine	Shut	Lash	Rash
Shone	Shook	Sash	Rush

It will be observed that the prefixed and the suffixed SH
has approximately the same whispered sound.

14. TH. The tongue is used to give the hard palate a pronounced impetus in the delivery of this digraph. It covers
the hard palate in an all-encompassing manner. There
must be good diaphragmatic support for a resonant TH.
Actually the breathy escape follows the tongue action
against the roof of the mouth.

Thin	Through	Birth	Death
Think	Three	Fifth	Warmth
Thump	Myth		

The pitch resonation of the consonant TH is always below
that of the vowel in the word of which it is a part. Both
the choral director and singer must be sure to attack the
digraph TH at the pitch level of the vowel to be sung.

<u>Lesson Twenty</u> Consonants Requiring Pronounced Palate Action.

1. <u>K</u>. The <u>K</u> requires firm diaphragmatic support. It must possess a vigorous closed palatal propulsion in the roof of the mouth. The teeth are separated and the lips drawn apart. Its delivery requires an energized stroke or propulsion of energy if it is to receive good articulation.

Kind	Pick	Nickel
Kink	Tick	
Kick	Nick	

2. <u>G</u>. Like <u>K</u>, the consonant <u>G</u> requires good diaphragmatic support. Like <u>K</u>, the palatal area is closed off in preparation for its delivery. When <u>G</u> is delivered there is a rumbling resonation. The consonant cannot be delivered unless it is followed by a vowel. Thus, <u>G</u> equals (G-ee). It, too, must be delivered with preciseness, or the <u>G</u> will become breathy and of poor quality.

Ground	Got
Grail	Grain
Go	Grab

3. <u>X</u>. The <u>X</u> actually has the phonetics of ĕ-k-s. The mouth is comfortably opened with the lips drawn backwards. The consonant should not be drawn out because of the breathy hissing sound that will conclude its final delivery. Crispness must characterize its emission.

Box	Nixon
Fix	Dixon
Next	Six

<u>Lesson Twenty-One</u>   Evidences of Consonantal Obstructions to Tonal
and Textual Delivery.

  In passing from one syllable ending to the beginning of the
next, it is imperative that each consonant delivery be made so that
the jaw is not in the way for good tonal and textual delivery.   With
the delivery of consonants the singer must be sure to study the action of the jaw to see whether it is unnecessarily closing upon the
purveyors of tone, which the consonants and the vowels actually become.   It has already been said that the tongue and the lips assume
the major action of vowel and consonant delivery.   The jaw plays
but a secondary role.

  The English phrase "None else can deliver us" is replete
with opportunities for aiding and modifying jaw action, so that the
maximum flow of <u>vowel tone</u> will not be unduly obstructed.   Most inexperienced singers will keep the jaw opening and shutting at the beginning and ending of each word.   The only <u>real</u> tonal stop in this
phrase is the dental (percussive) in the word <u>deliver</u>.   It is true
that many of the consonants nearly close the mouth, but every effort
should be made to keep the jaw separated.

GLORY TO GOD IN THE HIGHEST
For Chorus of Mixed Voices (SATB)
a cappella

LUKE 2:14   CLINTON ELLIOTT

In the illustration from Elliott's "Glory To God In The Highest" be sure that the G in Glory is articulated as a velar or soft-palate sound. It should not require the mouth to be completely closed before the delivery of the G. Let the soft-palate area be initiated into action, but do not have the mouth completely closed before the emission of the G's.

The phrase, "Holy Saviour, who takest upon Thee the sins of mortals," offers an excellent illustration for observing our previous cautions. In the word "Holy" the aspirate H can be produced without closing the jaw. Let us suppose that there was a series of words starting with H, such as in the song, "Holy, Holy, Holy," the sequence of H's can be produced without closing the jaw. Let the H pass through the mouth, sustain the vowel o as long as possible, and deliver the consonant l with good tongue action without disturbing the jaw. Every consonant and vowel does not need munching.

Another phrase, "The Big Bear and the Little Bear," has the consonant B repeated three times. It is an explosive consonant; sound B and you'll notice that it is voiced. The lips are necessary and must come together in the production of B; thus the mouth is temporarily closed. This letter is in sharp contrast to our previous illustrations. The consonant must, however, be articulated precisely and fast.

An attempt has been made to show contrasts in needless consonantal obstructions and those that necessarily impede tonal flow. Enough of the problem has been indicated so that the singer can be aware of needless obstructions to good tonal delivery and can guard against such errors.

The Aspirated H and Tone. The anticipated and aspirated H
is one of the most common errors which is superimposed on textual
delivery. Conductors listen for those errors for which they have
been trained to hear or by experience have found to be disturbing
to a musical performance. Very often a critical reviewer can detect the disconcerting effects of the anticipated H as shown in the
following illustrations:

George F. Handel "Glory to God" (From The Messiah). (Rockville
Centre, L.I., New York: Belwin, Inc., Octavo 1161. Copyright
1952). Used by permission of the publishers, Belwin, Inc., New
York, N.Y.

The Lord is My Strength

Anthem for Mixed Voices S.A.T.B.

Helen Jun Marth   "The Lord Is My Strength." (Rockville Centre, L.I., N.Y.: Belwin, Inc., 1952.) Copyright 1952 by Belwin, Inc. Permission granted.

George F. Handel   "For Unto Us a Child Is Born" (From The Messiah). (Rockville Centre, L.I., New York: Belwin, Inc., Octavo
1160). Used by permission of the publishers, Belwin, Inc., New
York, N.Y.

Another disconcerting yet ever prevalent manifestation of the
anticipated H is to be found in the singing of the well-known carol,
"The First Noel." It little matters how the word Noel is spelled;
be it Noel or Nowell. In the refrain there are a series of Nowells.
Without fail, the hearer will hear No (h) ell, No (h) ell, No (h) ell.
By calling the singer's attention to what is being done, the error can
be corrected. There must be a mental hesitancy of thought delivery

requiring a dramatic emphasis on "well" or "el." The <u>H</u> will then
be more easily eliminated.   There are many words where the <u>H</u> is
anticipated at the beginning of words, or it is superimposed on sustained words in moving sequences of notes when but one syllable is
used. Note the following phrase:

"Blessed forever more." (Rockville Centre, L.I., New York:
Belwin, Octavo 1163. Copyright 1952). Used by permission of the
publishers, Belwin, Inc., New York, N.Y.

In "Inflamatus et Accensus" by Rossini will be found the following opportunity for constantly repeating the <u>H</u> in the melodic rise of the
phraseline. It is vocal superimposition which vocalists feel (unconsciously) assists them in negotiating the vocal phrase which is quite
difficult.

G. Rossini "Inflamatus et Accensus." (Rockville Centre, L.I., N.Y.: Belwin, Octavo 1159. Copyright 1952). 7. Used by permission of the publishers, Belwin, Inc., New York, N.Y.

And again in the same example the phrase "there to worship with the faithful" the <u>H</u> is superimposed on the word when the singer raises the syllable <u>wor</u> up to the sequential pitch (E-flat) (sh (H) ip) as indicated in the following:

<u>Tone Quality and Textual Problems</u>. It is common that composers may have a theoretical command of music. It is also well known that composers seemingly often ignore the vocal-textual demands in their writing. Particularly is this true with song literature for the very high and the very low voices. A series of bright vowels on very high notes will cause great concern to the choral director. From inexperienced singers will issue much hideous tone. Take the soprano solo passage in Watts' "Nativity Carol" for illustrative purposes.

Watts   "Folk Nativity Carol." (Rockville Centre, L.I., New York:
Belwin, Octavo 1220, Copyright 1952).   Used by permission of the
publishers, Belwin, Inc., New York, N.Y.

It is obvious that the phrase, "Heav'n-ly blessings without number,"
is laden with a series of bright vowels.   They are ĕh, ē, ĕh, ĭh,
ĭh, ĭh.   For an inexperienced and poorly trained singer, that phrase
would be musically disastrous.   Another illustration, entitled, "A
Mother" can be found on the following page.

A Mother

For Women's Voices S.A.

Lois Rhea   "A Mother." (Rockville Centre, L.I., New York:
Belwin, Octavo 1243, Copyright 1952).   Used by permission of the
publishers, Belwin, Inc., New York, N.Y.

The phrase "God sought to give the sweetest thing," has some bright
vowels, but they are confined to the staff.   The pure ē, in "sweetest," will bear watching.   If that vowel is negotiated with good quality, the ĕh, of "est" should be relatively simple.   Very often the
bright vowels in the higher tessitura are ruined because they are
sung with mouth resonance above the limits designed for such areas
of the vocal range.

One passage for soprano solo, from Rossini's 'Inflamatus et

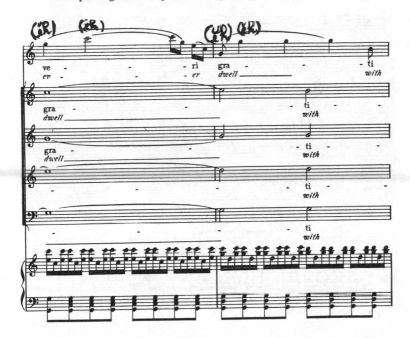

G. Rossini   "Inflamatus et Accensus." (Rockville Centre, L.I.,
New York: Belwin, Octavo 1159, Copyright 1952).   Used by permission of the publishers, Belwin, Inc., New York, N.Y.

Accensus," "ever dwell with thee," contains a series of bright
vowels in a particularly high tessitura sequence.   The ever expected
tonal yell is always looked for by the critical ear.

In the chorus accompaniment to this great Rossini solo will
be found a tenor passage which frequently is tonally very ineffective.
The tenors will spread the bright vowel "eh" of the word "dwell,"
and invariably scoop the four pitches of the high tessitura in the
second measure of the excerpts as indicated on the following page.

Lesson Twenty-Two   Exercises Emphasizing the Presence of Voiced
                    and Non-Voiced Consonants.

This study of the consonants classifies them as either voiced
or non-voiced.   Too frequently the choral director and singer are
not fully aware of frequency with which they may be found in verse.

In Lessons Seventeen through Twenty were indicated by classification and function the voiced and non-voiced consonants which
play an important part in facilitating the singer's diction.   They
were classified as follows:

Voiced	Voiceless
B, M, N, L, R, G or J, D,	F, K, P, Q, S, T, H, C, X
V, W, Y, and Z	

These twenty-one consonants added to the five vowels comprise the
letters of the English alphabet.

An analysis of the following excerpts from poetry indicates
the number of voiced and non-voiced consonants appearing in them.

"When I Am Dead, My Dearest"
by Christina Georgina Rossetti

Illus. I
```
W H E N  I  A M  D E A D,  M Y  D E A R E S T
v aV v  V  V V v  vVVv,  v  l  v  VVvVl l
S I N G  N O  S A D  S O N G S,  F O R  M E
lVvv   vV  lVv l  Vvvl,  lVv   vV
```

Legend: v   equals voiced
          l   equals non-voiced
          V   equals vowels
          a   equals aspirate

In the above illustration there are 16 voiced consonants out
of 25 consonants.
Resumé of the two lines of verse: 1 aspirate consonant;
14 vowels; 8 non-voiced consonants; 39 letters in the two
verses.

"Recessional"

by Rudyard Kipling

<u>Illus. II</u>

G O D   O F   O U R   F A T H E R S,
v V v   V l   V V v   l V l   a V v l
K N O W N   O F   O L D
l v V v v   V l   V v v
L O R D   O F   O U R   F A R   F L U N G
v V v v   V l   V V v   l V v   l v V v v
B A T T L E - L I N E
v V l l v V   v V v V

There are: 52 letters; 21 voiced consonants; 11 non-voiced
consonants; 19 vowels; 1 aspirate.

"When We Two Parted"

by Lord Byron

<u>Illus. III</u>

W H E N   W E   T W O   P A R T E D
v a V v   v V l   v V l   V v l V v
I N   S I L E N C E   A N D   T E A R S,
V v   l V v V v l V   V v v   l V V v l

There are: 32 letters; 12 voiced consonants; 7 non-voiced
consonants; 12 vowels; 1 aspirate.

These three excerpts indicate the considerable number of
voiced consonants that possess tonal sustainment. It is this property
which makes them "singable." By grouping together the vowels and
voiced consonants to be found in any of these verses, it is obvious
that these purveyors of tone when properly treated should immeasurably enhance the effectiveness of any singer's tone.
Of extreme importance to the effectiveness of a singer's tonal

Diction   155

pitch in the singing of voiced consonants is the observance that:
1) voiced consonants prefixing a word must be sung at the same
pitch as the vowel sound in the word that is to be sung; 2) voiced
consonants found at the end of a word must be sung at the pitch of
the vowel that precedes them.

Even those singers who recognize the importance of the vowel
in the development of good tone quality too frequently forget that it
is the vowel coupled with the consonant, that can, if properly used,
become the media for making effective and beautiful tone. The pre-
ceding discussion on diction, if continually and intelligently pursued,
will aid the singer in realizing an effective singing tone. The successful choral directors and singers are usually persons who pursue
a fundamental choral singing technique such as good diction until
they have mastered it. An abundance of evidence indicates, however, that there are few singers who understand the relationship
that exists between good diction, tone quality, and effective vocal
performance.

Bibliography

Anderson, Virgil A. Training the Speaking Voice. (New York: Oxford University Press, 1961).

Bach, A.B. The Art of Singing. (London: William Blackwood and Sons, 1886).

Breare, W.H. Vocal Faults and Their Remedies. (New York: G.P. Putnam's Sons, 1907).

Coffin, Berton The Singer's Repertoire. (New Brunswick, N.J.: The Scarecrow Press, 1956).

Crowest, Frederick J. Advice to Singers. (London: Frederick Warne and Co., 1892).

Curtis, H. Holbrook Voice Building and Tone Placing. (New York: D. Appleton and Co., 1901).

Davison, Archibald T. Choral Conducting. (Cambridge, Massachusetts: Harvard University Press, 1948).

Dawson, John J. The Voice of the Boy. (Chicago: Laidlaw Brothers, 1919).

Dickinson, A.E.F. The Art of J.S. Bach. (London, W. C. 1.: Hinrichsen Edition Limited, 1950).

Duey, Philip A. Bel Canto in its Golden Age. (New York: King's Crown Press, 1951).

Evetts, Edgar T. and Worthington, Robert A. The Mechanics of Singing. (London: J.M. Dent and Sons, Ltd., 1928).

Fillebrown, Thomas Resonance in Singing and Speaking. (New York-Boston: Oliver Ditson Co., 1906).

Finck, Henry T. Songs and Song Writers. (New York: Charles Scribner's Sons, 1901).

Francis, W. Nelson The English Language. (New York: W.W. Norton & Co., 1965).

Fuhr, Hayes M. Fundamentals of Choral Expression. (Lincoln:

University of Nebraska, 1944).

Gesheidt, Adelaide Make Singing a Joy. (New York: R. L. Hunt-
zinger, Inc., 1930).

Guttman, Oska Gymnastics of the Voice and Cure of Stuttering and
Stammering. (New York: Edgar S. Werner & Co., 1893).

Hall, John Walter and Brown, Ralph M. What Every Singer Should
Know. (Youngstown, Ohio: Vocal Science Publishing Company, 1928).

Haslam, W.E. Style in Singing. (New York: G. Schirmer, Inc.,
1911).

Hawn, Henry Gaines Diction For Singers and Composers. (New
York: Carnegie Hall, 1911).

Heilman, Arthur W. Phonics in Proper Perspective. (Columbus,
Ohio: Charles E. Merrill Publishing Co., 1964).

Henderson, W.J. The Art of the Singer. (New York: Charles
Scribner's Sons, 1906).

Herman, R.L. An Open Door For Singers. (New York: G.
Schirmer, Inc., 1912).

Howerton, George Technique and Style in Choral Singing. (New
York: Carl Fischer, Inc., 1957).

Huls, Helen Steen The Adolescent Voice. (New York: Vantage
Press, 1957).

Jacobs, Ruth Krehbiel The Successful Children's Choir. (Chicago:
H.T. FitzSimons Co., Inc., 1953).

Jacque, Reginald Voice-Training in Schools. (London: Oxford University Press, 1945).

Johnson, Claude E. Training of Boys' Voices. (Philadelphia:
Oliver Ditson Company, 1935).

Lehmann, Lilli How To Sing. (New York: The Macmillan Co.,
1903).

Lunn, Charles Philosophy of Voice. (Ninth Edition) (New York:
G. Schirmer, Inc., 1900).

McKensie, Duncan Training the Boy's Changing Voice. (New
Brunswick, New Jersey: Rutgers University Press, 1956).

Manser, Ruth B. Speech Correction on the Contract Plan. (Engle-
wood Cliffs, N.J.: Prentice-Hall, Inc., 1951).

Marchesi, Mathilde Ten Singing Lessons. (New York: Harper &
      Brother, 1901).

Miller, Frank E. Vocal Art-Science. (New York: G. Schirmer,
      Inc., 1917).

Morse, Frank E. A Graded List of Studies and Songs for Singing
      Teachers and Singers. (Boston: Charles W. Homeyer &
      Co., 1904).

Myer, Edmund J. Vocal Reinforcement (A Practical Study). (New
      York: American Publishing Co., 1891).

Nicoff, Irene and Dennis, Charles M. Simplified Vocal Training.
      (New York: Carl Fischer, Inc., 1940).

O'Neil, James Milton and Weaver, Andrew Thomas. The Elements
      of Speech. (New York: Longmans, Green and Co., 1926).

Pierce, Anne E. and Liebling, Estelle Class Lessons in Singing.
      (Morristown, New Jersey: Silver Burdett Co., 1937).

Pitts, Carol Pitts Voice Class Method. (Chicago: Neil A. Kjos
      Music Co., 1936).

Rogers, Clara Kathleen English Diction. Part I: The Voice in
      Speech. (Boston: 309 Beacon Street, 1915).

_____. The Philosophy of Singing. (New York: Harper &
      Brothers, 1898).

Rorke, Genevieve. Choral Teaching at the Junior High School Level.
      (Chicago: Hall & McCreary Co., 1947).

Russell, Louis Arthur English Diction for Singers and Speakers.
      (Boston: Oliver Ditson Co., 1905).

Shakespeare, William The Art of Singing. (Boston: Oliver Ditson
      Co., 1898).

Sieber, Ferdinand The Art of Singing. (New York: William A.
      Pond & Co., 1872).

Stanley, Douglas and Maxfield, P. The Voice and Its Production and
      Reproduction. (New York: Pitman Publishing Corporation,
      1933).

Staton, J. Frederic Sweet Singing In The Choir. (Toronto, Canada:
      Irwin and Company, Ltd., 1942).

Sunderman, Lloyd Frederick Some Techniques for Choral Success.
      (Rockville Centre, L.I.: Belwin, Inc., 1952).

Sunderman, Lloyd Frederick Organization of the Church Choir.
(Rockville Centre, L.I.: Belwin, Inc., 1957).

_____. The Primary Choir. (Chicago: Summy Publishing
Co., 1957).

_____. Basic Vocal Instructor. (Rockville Centre, L.I.:
Belwin, Inc., 1958).

Weaver, Andrew Thomas Speech. (New York: Longmans, Green
and Co., 1942).

Westerman, Kenneth N. Emergent Voice. 2nd ed. (Ann Arbor,
Michigan: Box 62; Privately Published, 1955).

Wilcke, Eva German Diction in Singing. (New York: E.P. Dutton
& Co., Inc., 1930).

Wilson, Harry Robert Artistic Choral Singing. (New York: G.
Schirmer, Inc., 1959).

Winn, Cyril Children Singing. (New York: Oxford University
Press, 1952).